Travels, chiefly on foot, through several parts of England, in 1782. Described in letters to a friend, by Charles P. Moritz, a literary gentleman of Berlin. Translated from the German, by a lady.

Karl Philipp Moritz

PRINT EDITIONS

Travels, chiefly on foot, through several parts of England, in 1782. Described in letters to a friend, by Charles P. Moritz, a literary gentleman of Berlin. Translated from the German, by a lady.

Moritz, Karl Philipp

ESTCID: T180049

Reproduction from Bodleian Library (Oxford)

Translated from 'Reisen eines Deutschen in England im Jahre 1782', Berlin, 1783.

London : printed for G. G. and J. Robinson, 1795.

xviii,269,[1]p. ; 12°

Eighteenth Century
Collections Online
Print Editions

Gale ECCO Print Editions

Relive history with *Eighteenth Century Collections Online*, now available in print for the independent historian and collector. This series includes the most significant English-language and foreign-language works printed in Great Britain during the eighteenth century, and is organized in seven different subject areas including literature and language; medicine, science, and technology; and religion and philosophy. The collection also includes thousands of important works from the Americas.

The eighteenth century has been called "The Age of Enlightenment." It was a period of rapid advance in print culture and publishing, in world exploration, and in the rapid growth of science and technology – all of which had a profound impact on the political and cultural landscape. At the end of the century the American Revolution, French Revolution and Industrial Revolution, perhaps three of the most significant events in modern history, set in motion developments that eventually dominated world political, economic, and social life.

In a groundbreaking effort, Gale initiated a revolution of its own: digitization of epic proportions to preserve these invaluable works in the largest online archive of its kind. Contributions from major world libraries constitute over 175,000 original printed works. Scanned images of the actual pages, rather than transcriptions, recreate the works *as they first appeared.*

Now for the first time, these high-quality digital scans of original works are available via print-on-demand, making them readily accessible to libraries, students, independent scholars, and readers of all ages.

For our initial release we have created seven robust collections to form one the world's most comprehensive catalogs of 18th century works.

Initial Gale ECCO Print Editions collections include:

History and Geography
Rich in titles on English life and social history, this collection spans the world as it was known to eighteenth-century historians and explorers. Titles include a wealth of travel accounts and diaries, histories of nations from throughout the world, and maps and charts of a world that was still being discovered. Students of the War of American Independence will find fascinating accounts from the British side of conflict.

Social Science

Delve into what it was like to live during the eighteenth century by reading the first-hand accounts of everyday people, including city dwellers and farmers, businessmen and bankers, artisans and merchants, artists and their patrons, politicians and their constituents. Original texts make the American, French, and Industrial revolutions vividly contemporary.

Medicine, Science and Technology

Medical theory and practice of the 1700s developed rapidly, as is evidenced by the extensive collection, which includes descriptions of diseases, their conditions, and treatments. Books on science and technology, agriculture, military technology, natural philosophy, even cookbooks, are all contained here.

Literature and Language

Western literary study flows out of eighteenth-century works by Alexander Pope, Daniel Defoe, Henry Fielding, Frances Burney, Denis Diderot, Johann Gottfried Herder, Johann Wolfgang von Goethe, and others. Experience the birth of the modern novel, or compare the development of language using dictionaries and grammar discourses.

Religion and Philosophy

The Age of Enlightenment profoundly enriched religious and philosophical understanding and continues to influence present-day thinking. Works collected here include masterpieces by David Hume, Immanuel Kant, and Jean-Jacques Rousseau, as well as religious sermons and moral debates on the issues of the day, such as the slave trade. The Age of Reason saw conflict between Protestantism and Catholicism transformed into one between faith and logic -- a debate that continues in the twenty-first century.

Law and Reference

This collection reveals the history of English common law and Empire law in a vastly changing world of British expansion. Dominating the legal field is the *Commentaries of the Law of England* by Sir William Blackstone, which first appeared in 1765. Reference works such as almanacs and catalogues continue to educate us by revealing the day-to-day workings of society.

Fine Arts

The eighteenth-century fascination with Greek and Roman antiquity followed the systematic excavation of the ruins at Pompeii and Herculaneum in southern Italy; and after 1750 a neoclassical style dominated all artistic fields. The titles here trace developments in mostly English-language works on painting, sculpture, architecture, music, theater, and other disciplines. Instructional works on musical instruments, catalogs of art objects, comic operas, and more are also included.

The BiblioLife Network

This project was made possible in part by the BiblioLife Network (BLN), a project aimed at addressing some of the huge challenges facing book preservationists around the world. The BLN includes libraries, library networks, archives, subject matter experts, online communities and library service providers. We believe every book ever published should be available as a high-quality print reproduction; printed on-demand anywhere in the world. This insures the ongoing accessibility of the content and helps generate sustainable revenue for the libraries and organizations that work to preserve these important materials.

The following book is in the "public domain" and represents an authentic reproduction of the text as printed by the original publisher. While we have attempted to accurately maintain the integrity of the original work, there are sometimes problems with the original work or the micro-film from which the books were digitized. This can result in minor errors in reproduction. Possible imperfections include missing and blurred pages, poor pictures, markings and other reproduction issues beyond our control. Because this work is culturally important, we have made it available as part of our commitment to protecting, preserving, and promoting the world's literature.

GUIDE TO FOLD-OUTS MAPS and OVERSIZED IMAGES

The book you are reading was digitized from microfilm captured over the past thirty to forty years. Years after the creation of the original microfilm, the book was converted to digital files and made available in an online database.

In an online database, page images do not need to conform to the size restrictions found in a printed book. When converting these images back into a printed bound book, the page sizes are standardized in ways that maintain the detail of the original. For large images, such as fold-out maps, the original page image is split into two or more pages

Guidelines used to determine how to split the page image follows:

• Some images are split vertically; large images require vertical and horizontal splits.
• For horizontal splits, the content is split left to right.
• For vertical splits, the content is split from top to bottom.
• For both vertical and horizontal splits, the image is processed from top left to bottom right.

CHIEFLY ON FOOT,

THROUGH

SEVERAL PARTS OF ENGLAND,

IN

1782.

DESCRIBED

IN LETTERS TO A FRIEND,

BY CHARLES P. MORITZ,

A LITERARY GENTLEMAN OF BERLIN.

TRANSLATED FROM THE GERMAN,

BY A LADY.

LONDON.

PRINTED FOR C. G. AND J. ROBINSON, PATER-NOSTER-ROW.

1795.

PREFACE,

By the EDITOR.

———

ONE of the moſt diſtinguiſhing features in the literary hiſtory of our age and country, is the paſſion of the public for voyages and travels. Of the books that have lately been publiſhed, there are none, novels alone excepted, that, in point of number, bear any proportion to them. A ſpot on the globe can hardly be named, whither ſome of our adventurous countrymen have not penetrated, and with a public ſpirit, and a degree of benevolence hardly inferior to their courage, what they have ſeen, they have publiſhed. Firſt encouraged and promoted by royal munificence, it is equally to the credit of the

A 2   Sovereign

Sovereign and his subjects, that both travelling, and the writing of travels, have become fashionable; and the prevailing objects of the public taste. Such has been our national partiality to travellers and travelling, that there are instances of enterprising and benevolent men, who have visited foreign countries, merely that they might inform their countrymen what they heard and saw: nay, some have been so anxious to gratify this national curiosity, that more than one well-received and useful book of travels might be named, written by persons who never were travellers.

A similar taste actuated the people of France, as long as they continued to be a civilized people. Our rivals in every thing, they also were the only people, who had any pretentions to vie with us either as travellers, or the writers of travels.

travels. But, it is not mere national vanity to ſay, that the Engliſh, now at leaſt, far excel the French both in the quantity and quality, of their books of travels. It does not ſeem difficult to account for this. The French, in general, are ſo well ſatisfied with themſelves, that, where no political intereſts intervene, they are ſeldom much intereſted about any other people · and they travel and write their travels, not ſo much with any view of improving themſelves, or their countrymen, as to be gratified by an opportunity of diſplaying their ſuperiority to all other nations. It is fair to ſuppoſe alſo, that, like moſt other nations, they really have leſs curioſity, than has always marked the character of Engliſhmen. Still, it needs neither to be denied or concealed, that many Frenchmen have been great travellers, and have alſo publiſhed

many

many valuable books of travels. It is remarkable, however, that whilst many Britons, who have rambled but a few weeks in France, have been so obliging on their return as to favour their country-men with a full and true account of all that they had heard and feen during their peregrinations, hardly any Frenchman has even given any account (and certainly not any good account) of thefe king-doms. If Frenchmen who, more than any other nation, vifited England, have feldom thought it worth their while to tell the world what they thought of us and our country, it was ftill lefs to be expected from the inhabitants of other countries; who, if not lefs in the habit of travel-ling, are certainly lefs in the habit of publifhing their travels.

It may feem, perhaps, to abate a little of that ftrong idea of French vanity,

with

with which it is hardly poſſible for Engliſhmen not to be impreſſed, to own, as impartiality requires we ſhould, that the accounts which natives of France have given of their own kingdom do not, probably, much exceed thoſe given of it by natives of Great-Britain, either in minuteneſs or accuracy, or even in number. Theſe tours into France, however, or any other foreign tours, bear no proportion to the almoſt countleſs number of excurſions and deſcriptions, given not only of our iſland in general, but of almoſt every particular part of it, by Britons. So copious indeed are theſe publications, that the valetudinarian, or the inactive man, may now, at his eaſe, obtain full and exact information of every place, and every circumſtance relative to our local hiſtory, without ſtirring from his own fire-ſide.

It

It is natural for every man to be partial to that country which he has the happinefs to call his own . and for a native
of this favoured land, not to be confcious
of its fuperior value is fomething worfe
than ftupidity. Still, however, it is neceffary, proper, and defirable for the
people of any country not to form their
judgments of themfelves entirely by their
own obfervations ; but to learn and know
what opinions and what judgments are
formed of them by perfons, who cannot
be fufpected of being under any undue
bias. It is particularly proper for Englifhmen, who have fo long allowed themfelves the great liberty of giving their
unreferved opinions of others. But,
amidft all our ftores of domeftic, as well
as travelling anecdotes, fuch a view of
England feems to be ftill a defideratum.

That the humble volume now fubmitted,

mitted, with all poffible deference to the candour of the Englifh nation, in an Englifh drefs, will fill up this gap in the literary hiftory of the times, it might perhaps be deemed prefumption confidently to fuppofe. All that the Editor of it ventures to hint on the fubject, is, that it contributes fomething towards it: and that though this hafty fketch of our metropolis, and this fhort tour through a part of our kingdom by a Foreigner, be far enough from being fuch an one as he could have wifhed to have brought forward, and would have brought forward, had there been a choice, it is the only one of the kind of a recent date, that he has happened to fee. And though he is aware, that its contents are not of a nature likely to command a very general attention, and certainly not fuch as a profeffed book-maker, in the habit of

A 5

catering

catering for the public taſte, would have provided, yet is it not without merit, and merit of a kind particularly entitled to the reſpect of Engliſhmen.

Beſides the more obvious advantages likely to reſult from our occaſionally liſtening to the remarks and opinions of other travellers, than thoſe alone of France and our own country, it might not perhaps be without its uſe ſometimes to conſult them, if it were only on the ſcore of compoſition. There is a manner of thinking, and a ſtile of writing, peculiar to every nation. An Engliſhman, for inſtance, would no more think of deſcribing a country, or a people, with the minute prolixity of Germans in general, than he would of criticiſing a work of taſte with the phlegm of a Dutch commentator, or with the elaborate and cloſe preciſion of an argument on a

theological

theological thesis. Yet whilst we thus confine ourselves entirely to our own modes, it is possible we may overlook many little latent improprieties in our writings, to which custom now reconciles us; but which, it is probable, would be apparent to us, by being compared with the similar writings of a different nation. By bringing our writings to this test, we should learn perhaps, that though we do already excel, we may yet be more excellent. That, in general, our books of travels are superior to those of most other people, will be contested by no competent judges; but, it by no means follows, that we have attained the acme of perfection in this species of writing. One glaring error into which our writers of travels, as well as the writers of history, have fallen, the editor hopes to be pardoned for mentioning; because, as

A 6 he

he is neither a traveller, nor an author,
he cannot well be fufpected of being
prompted either by jealoufy or by envy.
It is no longer fufficient, that a book is
inftructive and ufeful, it muft alfo be entertaining : and hence, books of travels
might be named, and hiftories too, written
fo much in the manner and character of
novels, as actually to have become ftock-
books on the fhelves of circulating libraries.   There cannot be a more degrading
condefcenfion, than it is for writers of
abilities thus meanly to flatter a falfe
tafte.   From this fault at leaft, the volume now prefented to the public, is
exempt.   Our German does not deal in
the marvellous ; neither does he affect
to be fentimental.   On a fine profpect, it
is to be owned, he loves to dwell, and
defcribe, with fome degree of rapture ;
but he does not bewilder either himfelf,

or

or his readers in the fairey fcencs of picturefque beauty. His matter is not always highly important, yet is it never beneath the notice of even a wife man; for, though we may perhaps but rarely admire his genius, we cannot but refpect his good fenfe.

Confidering to how many richer feafts of the kind we have lately been invited, that fome of the firft rate geniufes of our age have traverfed our kingdom, as it were, on purpofe to defcribe it, and that, as if their own immediate communications were not fufficiently alluring, their works have been ftill farther fet off by all the charms that the elegant art of engraving can give them, it may feem little lefs than prefumption to hope, that the wanderings on foot of a poor, obfcure, German paftor, from London into Derbyfhire, will attract many readers. It fhould

fhould be remembered, however, that good fenfe belongs exclufively to no age, profeffion or ftation ; and that good fenfe, when accompanied by good nature, will always be fure to engage attention. Both thefe qualities our traveller will be found to poffefs, in no ordinary degree. Even when he is miftaken, he appears to be an intelligent man ; and fo candid and mild, that even indignities have not provoked him to ufe a fingle fharp expreffion.

The work is faid to have been well received at Berlin, and in Germany in general ; a circumftance by no means beneath the notice of Britifh readers. For, it may deferve to be reflected on, whether this may not be one of the cafes, in which Foreigners are as likely to form a fair eftimate of a work, as we are. If they are not fo well acquainted with the fubjects of which it treats, they are alfo lefs

to

to be fufpected of prejudice.   Still, however, it is admitted, that, without any
impeachment of their judgments on either
fide, thofe parts may be deemed of moft
value to a German, which an Englifhman
thinks of the leaft.   To the former, for
inftance, it may be of fome moment
to know what reception Foreigners of all
defcriptions are likely to meet with in
England : but, what Englifhman can be
very anxious to know, how the land-
lords and landladies of low ale-houfes
deport themfelves towards an itinerant
Forcigner, of perhaps no very promifing
appearance ? And an attentive obferver of
human nature, whatever be his country
or fituation, will not be difpleafed to fee
men and things in fcenes and circumftances
which have hitherto efcaped his notice,
only, becaufe they are common.   If fome
of the incidents here related be, after all,

confeffedly

confeffedly infignificant, or even palpably erroneous, ftill it may not be without its ufe for us to reflect, that were many of our writers of travels, who have juftly acquired no ordinary celebrity among us, to be tried and judged of by perfons in the countries which they have defcribed, it is more than probable, that many of their accounts of things, which have been admired in England, would there be rejected as frivolous or falfe. It is obvious to remark, that any opinions formed by an hafty traveller, who tarrieth but a day, muft needs be formed at much hazard. When therefore the candid reader may find himfelf fometimes tempted to fmile at the fimplicity of this good-natured German, whofe hafty opinions of our people and our country could not but be oftentimes crude and inaccurate, let him alfo be juft enough to reflect,

that

that fuch muft be the cafe alfo with fenfible foreigners, when they read our
books of travels into their countries.

All that the Editor prefumes faither to
add, is, that the tranflation is the firft
performance of the kind of a very young
lady; whofe name, if it had been thought
proper to mention it, would be indifferent
to no lover of found and deep learning,
and exemplary piety. It is her pride, and
her confolation, to be one of the daugh-
ters of a venerable man, who is mentioned with all the refpect due to him in
the enfuing letters. And, young as fhe is,
this is not the firft time fhe has folicited
and obtained Britifh patronage, and
Britifh protection. And now, with all
the diffidence natural to her fex and her
years, fhe entreats, that this her maiden
effay in literature may be received as a
tender of her heart-felt gratitude. The
Editor

Editor has revifed the tranflation, which, though far from being fervile, or even always literal, he thinks fufficiently faithful. Some little ftiffneffes, it is poffible, may ftill remain : but it has been the aim of the tranflator, without departing from the fenfe of the author, to exprefs that fenfe in fuch a way as fhe fuppofed her author would have done, had he been of London, rather than of Berlin. And this aim fhe feems, in general, very happily to have accomplifhed.

TRAVELS,

TRAVELS,

&c. &c.

ON THE THAMES, 3IST, *MAY.*

AT length, my deareſt Gedike, I find myſelf ſafely landed on the happy ſhores of that country, a ſight of which has, for many years, been my moſt earneſt wiſh , and whither I have ſo often, in imagination, tranſported myſelf. A few hours ago, the green hills of England yet ſwam imperfectly before our eyes, ſcarcely perceptible in the diſtant horizon. they now unfold themſelves on either ſide, forming as it were a double Amphitheatre. The ſun burſts through the clouds, and gilds alternately the ſhrubs, and meadows, on the diſtant ſhores: and we now eſpy the tops of two maſts of ſhips juſt peeping above the ſurface of the deep.—What an aweful warning to adventurous men! We now ſail

B   cloſe

clofe by thofe very fands, (*the Goodwin*) where fo many unfortunate perfons have found their graves.

The fhores now regularly draw nearer to each other the danger of the voyage is over, and the feafon for enjoyment, unembittered by cares, commences. How do we feel ourfelves, we, who have long been wandering, as it were, in a boundlefs fpace, on having once more gained profpects, that are not without limits! I fhould imagine, our fenfations are fomewhat like thofe of the traveller, who traverfes the immeafurable deferts of America, when fortunately he obtains an hut wherein to fhelter himfelf, in thofe moments he certainly enjoys himfelf, nor does he then complain of its being too fmall. It is indeed the lot of man to be always circumfcribed to a narrow fpace, even when he wanders over the moft extenfive regions, even when the huge fea envelopes him all around, and wraps him clofe to its bofom, in the act, as it were, of fwallowing him up in a moment. ftill he is feparated, from all the circumjacent immenfity of fpace only by one fmall part, or infignificant portion, of that immenfity.

That

That portion of this space, which I now see surrounding me, is a most delightful selection from the whole of beautiful nature. Here is the *Thames* full of large and small ships, and boats, difperfed here and there, which are either failing on with us, or lying at anchor, and there the hills on either fide, clad with fo foft, and mild a green, as I have no where elfe ever feen equalled. The charming banks of the *Elbe*, which I fo lately quitted, are as much furpaffed by thefe fhores, as autumn is by fpring! I fee every where nothing but fertile and cultivated lands, and thofe living hedges which in England, more than in any other country, form the boundaries of the green cornfields, and give to the whole of the diftant country, the appearance of a large and majeftic garden. The neat villages and fmall towns, with fundry intermediate country feats, fuggeft ideas of profperity and opulence, which it is not poffible to defcribe.

The profpect towards Gravefend is particularly beautiful. It is a clever little town, built on the fide of an hill, about which there lie hill and dale, and meadows, and arable land, intermixed with pleafure-grounds and

country

country feats; all diverfified in the moft agree-able manner.   On one of the higheft of thefe hills near Gravefend ftands a wind-mill, which is a very good object, as you fee it at fome diftance, as well as part of the country around it, on the windings of the Thames.   But as few human pleafures are ever complete and perfect, we too, amidft the pleafing con-templation of all thefe beauties, found our-felves expofed, on the quarter-deck, to un-commonly cold and piercing weather.   An unintermitting violent fhower of rain has driven me into the cabin, where I am now endeavouring to divert a gloomy hour, by given you the defcription of a pleafing one.

LONDON, 2D, JUNE.

THIS morning thofe of us who were fellow paffengers together in the great cabin, being fix in number, requefted to be fet on fhore, in a boat, a little before the veffel got to Dartford, which is ftill fixteen miles from London. This expedient is generally adopted, inftead of going up the Thames, towards London, where, on account of the aftonifhing number of fhips, which are always more crouded together the nearer you approach the city, it frequently requires many days before a fhip can finifh her paffage. He therefore who wifhes to lofe no time unnccceffarily, and wifhes alfo to avoid other inconveniences, fuch as frequent ftoppages, and, perhaps, fome alarming dafhings againft other fhips, prefers travelling thofe few miles by land in a poft chaife, which is not very expenfive, efpecially when three join together, as three paffengers pay no more than one. This indulgence is allowed by Act of Parliament.

As we left the veffel we were honoured with a general huzza, or, in the Englifh phrafe, with *three cheers,* echoed from the

B 3   German

German sailors of our ship. This nautical style of bidding their friends farewel our Germans have learned from the English The cliff where we landed was white and chalky, and as the distance was not great, nor other means of conveyance at hand, we resolved to go on foot to Dartford, immediately on landing we had a pretty steep hill to climb, and, that gained, we arrived at the first English village, where an uncommon neatness in the structure of the houses, which in general are built with red bricks, and flat roofs, struck me with a pleasing surprize, especially when I compared them with the long, rambling, inconvenient, and singularly mean cottages of our peasants. We now continued our way through the different villages, each furnished with his staff, and thus exhibited no remote resemblance of a caravan. Some few people who met us seemed to stare at us, struck, perhaps, by the singularity of our dress, or the peculiarity of our manner of travelling. On our route we passed a wood where a troop of gypsies had taken up their abode, around a fire, under a tree. The country, as we continued to advance, became more and more beautiful. Naturally,

perhaps,

perhaps, the earth is every where pretty much alike, but how different is it rendered by art! How different is that on which I now tread from ours, and every other spot I have ever feen.——The foil is rich even to exuberance, the verdure of the trees and hedges, in fhort the whole of this paradifaical region is without a parallel! The roads too are incomparable; I am aftonifhed how they have got them fo firm and folid, every ftep I took I felt, and was confcious, it was Englifh ground on which I trod.

We breakfafted at Dartford Here, for the firft time, I faw an Englifh foldier, in his red uniform, his hair cut fhort and combed back on his forehead, fo as to afford a full view of his fine broad manly face. Here too I firft faw (what I deemed a true Englifh fight) in the ftreet two boys boxing.

Our little party now feparated, and got into two poft-chaifes, each of which hold three perfons, though it muft be owned three cannot fit quite fo commodioufly in thefe chaifes as two, the hire of a poft chaife is a fhilling for every Englifh mile. They may be compared to our extra pofts, becaufe they are to be had at all times But thefe carriages are

very

very neat and lightly built, fo that you hardly perceive their motion, as they roll along thefe firm fmooth roads, they have windows in front, and on both fides. The horfes are generally good, and the poftillions particularly fmart and active, and always ride on a full trot. The one we had wore his hair cut fhort, a round hat, and a brown jacket, of tolerable fine cloth, with a nofegay in his bofom. Now and then, when he drove very hard, he looked round and with a fmile feemed to folicit our approbation. A thoufand charming fpots, and beautiful landfcapes, on which my eye would long have dwelt with rapture, were now rapidly paffed with the fpeed of an arrow.

Our road appeared to be undulatory, and our journey, like the journey of life, feemed to be a pretty regular alternation of up hill and down, and here and there it was diverfified with copfes and woods, the majeftic Thames, every now and then, like a little foreft of mafts, rifing to our view, and anon lofing itfelf among the delightful towns and villages. The amazing large figns which, at the entrance of villages, hang in the middle of the ftreet, being faftened to large beams, which

are

are extended acrofs the ftreet from one houfe to another oppofite to it, particularly ftruck me, thefe fign pofts have the appearance of gates, or of gateways, for which I at firft took them, but the whole apparatus, unneceffarily large as it feems to be, is intended for nothing more than to tell the inquifitive traveller that there is an inn. At length, ftunned as it were by this conftant rapid fucceffion of interefting objects to engage our attention, we arrived at Greenwich nearly in a ftate of ftupefaction.

The Profpect of London.

We firft defcry'd it enveloped in a thick fmoke, or fog St. Paul's arofe, like fome huge mountain, above the enormous mafs of fmaller buildings. The monument, a very lofty column erected in memory of the great fire of London, exhibited to us, perhaps, chiefly on account of its immenfe height, apparently fo difproportioned to its other dimenfion (for it actually ftruck us as refembling rather a flender maft, towering up in immeafurable height into the clouds, than as what it really is, a ftately obelifk) an unufual and fingular appearance. Still we went on,

B 5 and

and drew nearer and nearer with amazing velocity, and the furrounding objects became every moment more diftinct. Weftminfter Abbey, the Tower, a fteeple, one church and then another, prefented themfelves to our view, and we could now plainly diftinguifh the high round chimnies, on the tops of the houfes, which yet feemed to us to form an innumerable number of fmaller fpires, or fteeples.

The road from Greenwich to London is actually bufier, and far more alive, than the moft frequented ftreets in Berlin, at every ftep we met people on horfeback, in carriages, and foot-paffengers; and every where alfo, and on each fide of the road, well-built and noble houfes, whilft all along, at proper diftances, the road was lined with lamp pofts. One thing in particular ftruck and furprifed me not a little, this was the number of people we met riding and walking with fpectacles on, among whom were many who appeared ftout, healthy, and young. We were ftopped at leaft three times at barriers, or gates, here called turnpikes, to pay a duty or toll which, however fmall, as being generally paid in their copper coinage, in the end amounted to fome fhillings.

At

At length we arrived at the magnificent bridge of Weſtminſter. The proſpect from this bridge alone ſeems to afford one, the epitome of a journey, or a voyage in miniature, as containing ſomething of every thing that moſt uſually occurs on a journey. It is a little aſſemblage of contraſts and contrarieties. In contraſt to the round, modern, and majeſtic Cathedral of St. Paul's, on your right, the venerable, old-faſhioned, and hugely noble, long, Abbey of Weſtminſter, with its enormous pointed roof, riſes on the left. Down the Thames, to the right, you ſee Blackfriar's Bridge, which does not yield much, if at all, in beauty, to that of Weſtminſter, on the left bank of the Thames are delightful terraces, planted with trees, and thoſe new taſteful buildings, called the Adelphi On the Thames itſelf are countleſs ſwarms of little boats paſſing and repaſſing, many with one maſt and one ſail, and many with none, in which perſons of all ranks are carried over. Thus, there is hardly leſs ſtir and buſtle on this river, than there is in ſome of its own London's crouded ſtreets. Here, indeed, you no longer ſee great ſhips, for they come no farther than London-Bridge

We

We now drove-into the City, by Charing-Crofs, and along the Strand, to thofe very Adelphi Buildings, which had juft afforded us fo charming a profpect, on Weftminfter-Bridge.

My two travelling companions, both in the fhip and in the poft chaife, were two young Englifhmen, who living in this part of the town, obligingly offered me any affiftance and fervices in their power, and, in particular, to procure me a lodging the fame day in their neighbourhood.

In the ftreets through which we paffed, I muft own, the houfes in general ftruck me as if they were dark and gloomy, and yet, at the fame time, they alfo ftruck me as prodigioufly great, and majeftic. At that moment I could not, in my own mind, compare the external view of London with that of any other city I had ever before feen. But I remember, (and furely, it is fingular) that about five years ago on my firft entrance into Leipzig, I had the very fame fenfations I now felt. It is poffible, that the high houfes by which the ftreets at Leipzig are partly darkened, the great number of fhops and the croud of people, fuch as till then I had never feen,

might

might have some faint resemblance with the scene now surrounding me in London.

There are every where leading from the Strand to the Thames some well-built, lesser, or subordinate streets, of which the Adelphi-Buildings are now, by far, the foremost. One district in this neighbourhood goes by the name of York-Buildings; and in this lies George-street, where my two travelling companions lived. There reigns in those smaller streets, towards the Thames, so pleasing a calm, compared to the tumult and bustle of people, and carriages, and horses, that are constantly going up and down the Strand, that in going into one of them you can hardly help fancying yourself removed at a distance from the noise of the City, even whilst the noisiest part of it is still so near at hand.

It might be about ten or eleven o'clock when we arrived here. After the two Englishmen had first given me some breakfast, at their lodgings, which consisted of tea and bread and butter, they went about with me themselves, in their own neighbourhood, in search of an apartment, which they at length procured for me, for sixteen shillings a week, at the house of a taylor's widow, who

lived

lived oppofite to them It was very fortunate, on other accounts, that they went with me, for, equipped as I was, having neither brought clean linen, nor change of cloaths from my trunk, I might, perhaps have found it difficult to obtain good lodgings.

It was a very uncommon, but pleafing fenfation I experienced, on being now, for the firft time in my life, entirely among Englifhmen, among people whofe language was foreign, their manners foreign, and in a foreign climate, with whom, notwithftanding, I could converfe as familiarly as though we had been educated together from our infancy. It is certainly an ineftimable advantage to underftand the language of the country through which you travel. I did not at firft give the people I was with any reafon to fufpect I could fpeak Englifh, but I foon found that the more I fpoke, the more attention and regard I met with. I now occupy a large room in front on the ground floor, which has a carpet and matts, and is very neatly furnifhed, the chairs are covered with leather, and the tables are of mahogany. Adjoining to this I have another large room I may do juft as I pleafe, and keep my own tea, coffee, bread

and

and butter; for which purpofe my landlady has given me a cupboard in my room, which locks up.

The family confifts of the miftrefs of the houfe, her maid and her two fons, *Jacky* and *Jerry*, fingular abbreviations for *John* and *Jeremiah*. The eldeft, Jacky, about twelve years old, is a very lively boy, and often entertains me in the moft pleafing manner, by relating to me his different employments at fchool, and afterwards defiring me, in my turn, to relate to him all manner of things about Germany. He repeats his *amo, amas, amavi*, in the fame finging tone as our common fchool-boys. As I happened once, when he was by, to hum a lively tune, he ftared at me with furprize, and then reminded me it was Sunday, and fo, that I might not forfeit his good opinion, by any appearance of levity, I gave him to underftand, that in the hurry of my journey, I had forgotten the day. He has already fhewn me St. James's Park, which is not far from hence, and now let me give you fome defcription of the renowned

St James's Park.

This Park is nothing more than a femi-circle

circle, formed of an alley of trees, which
enclofe a large green area, in the middle of
which is a marfhy pond.

The cows feed on this green turf, and their
milk is fold here on the fpot, quite new.

In all the alleys, or walks, there are
benches, where you may reft yourfelf   When
you come through the Horfe-Guards (which
is provided with feveral paffages) into the
Park, on the right hand is St James's Palace,
or the King's place of refidence, one of the
meaneft publick buildings in London.   At
the lower end, quite at the extremity, is the
Queen's Palace, an handfome and modern
building, but very much refembling a private
houfe.   As for the reft, there are generally
every where about St. James's Park very
good houfes, which is a great addition to it.
There is alfo before the femicircle of the
trees juft mentioned, a large vacant fpace,
where the foldiers are exercifed.

How little this famous park is to be compared with our park at Berlin I need not
mention.   And yet one cannot but form an
high idea of St. James's Park, and other
public places in London, this arifes, perhaps,
from their having been oftener mentioned in
romances

romances and other books than ours have. Even the squares and streets of London are more noted, and better known, than many of our principal towns.

But what again greatly compenfates for the mediocrity of this park, is the aftonifhing number of people who, towards evening, in fine weather, refort here, our fineft walks are never fo full even in the midft of fummer. The exquifite pleafure of mixing freely with fuch a concourfe of people, who are for the moft part well dreffed and handfome, I have experienced this evening for the firft time.

Before I went to the park I took another walk with my little *Jacky*, which did not coft me much fatigue, and yet was moft uncommonly interefting. I went down the little ftreet in which I live to the Thames; nearly at the end of it, towards the left, a few fteps led me to a fingularly pretty terrace, planted with trees, on the very brink of the river.

Here I had the moft delightful profpect you can poffibly imagine. Before me was the Thames with all its windings, and the ftately arches of its bridges; Weftminfter with its venerable Abbey to the right, to the left again London, with St. Paul's, feemed to

wind

wind all along the windings of the Thames;
and on the other side of the water lay Southwark, which is now also considered as part of
London   Thus, from this single spot, I could
nearly, at one view, see the whole City, at
least that side of it towards the Thames.   Not
far from hence, in this charming quarter of
the town, lived the renowned *Garrick*.   Depend upon it I shall often visit this delightful
walk, during my stay in London.

To day my two Englishmen carried me to
a neighbouring tavern,   or rather an eating-
house,   where we paid a shilling each for some
roast-meat, and a sallad, giving, at the same
time, nearly half as much to the waiter, and
yet this is reckoned a cheap house, and a
cheap stile of living.—But, I believe, for the
future, I shall pretty often dine at home, I
have already begun this evening with my
supper.   I am now sitting by the fire, in my
own room in London, the day is nearly at an
end, the first I have spent in England, and I
hardly know, whether I ought to call it only
one day, when I reflect what a quick and
varied succession of new and striking ideas
have, in so short a time, passed in my mind.

LONDON,

LONDON, 5TH, JUNE.

AT length, deareſt Gedike, I am again ſet-
tled, as I have now got my trunk and all my
things from the ſhip, which arrived only yeſterday. Not wiſhing to have it taken to the
Cuſtom-houſe, which occaſions a great deal
of trouble, I was obliged to give a douceur
to the officers, and thoſe who came on board
the ſhip, to ſearch it. Having pacified, as
I thought, one of them with a couple of
ſhillings, another came forward and proteſted
againſt the delivery of the trunk upon truſt,
till I had given him as much: to him ſuc-
ceeded a third; ſo that it coſt me ſix ſhillings, which I willingly paid, becauſe it
would have coſt me ſtill more at the Cuſtom-
houſe.

By the ſide of the Thames were ſeveral
porters, one of whom took my huge heavy
trunk on his ſhoulders with aſtoniſhing eaſe;
and carried it till I met a hackney-coach.
This I hired for two ſhillings, immediately
put the trunk into it, accompanying it myſelf, without paying any thing extra for my
own ſeat. This is a great advantage in the
Engliſh

English hackney-coaches, that you are allowed to take with you, whatever you please: for you thus save at least one half of what you must pay to a porter, and besides go with it yourself, and are better accommodated. The observations, and the expressions of the common people here have often struck me, as peculiar: they are generally laconic; but always much in earnest, and significant. When I came home, my landlady kindly recommended it to the coachman not to ask more than was just, as I was a foreigner: to which he answered, nay, if he were not a foreigner, I should not overcharge him

My letters of recommendation to a merchant here, which I could not bring with me on account of my hasty departure from Hamburgh, are also arrived. These have saved me a great deal of trouble in the changing of my money. I can now take my German money back to Germany; and when I return thither myself, refund to the correspondent of the merchant here, the sum which he here pays me in English money. I should otherwise have been obliged to sell my Prussian *Friedrick's d'or* for what they weigh'd. for some few Dutch dollars, which I was obliged

liged to part with, before I got this credit, they only gave me eight shillings.

A foreigner has here nothing to fear from being pressed as a sailor, unless indeed he should be found at any suspicious place. A singular invention for this purpose of pressing, is a ship which is placed on land not far from the Tower on Tower-hill, furnished with masts and all the appurtenances of a ship. The persons attending this ship promise simple country people, who happen to be standing and stareing at it, to shew it to them for a trifle; and as soon as they are in, they are secured as in a trap, and according to circumstances made sailors of, or let go again.

The footway paved with large stones on both sides of the streets, appears to a foreigner exceedingly convenient and pleasant, as one may there walk in perfect safety, in no more danger from the prodigious crowd of carts and coaches, than if one was in one's own room; for no wheel dares come a finger's breadth upon the curb-stone. However, politeness requires you to let a lady, or any one to whom you wish to shew respect, pass, not, as we do, always to the right, but on the side next the houses or the wall, whether that

that happens to be on the right, or on the
left, being deemed the safeft and moft convenient.   You feldom fee a perfon of any un-
derftanding or common fenfe, walk in the
middle of the ftreets in London, excepting
when they crofs over; which at Charing-
crofs and other places, where feveral ftreets
meet, is fometimes really dangerous.

It has a ftrange appearance, efpecially in
the Strand where there is a conftant fucceffion
of fhop after fhop, and where, not unfrequently, people of different trades inhabit
the fame houfe, to fee their doors, or the
tops of their windows, or boards exprefsly
for the purpofe, all written over from top to
bottom, with large painted letters.   Every
perfon, of every trade or occupation, who
owns ever fo finall a portion of an houfe,
makes a parade with a fign at his door, and
there is hardly a cobler, whofe name and
profeffion may not be read in large golden
characters, by every one that paffes. It is here
not at all uncommon to fee on doors in one
continued fucceffion, " *children educated here,*"
" *fhoes mended here,*" " *foreign fpirituous liquors
fold here,*" and " *Funerals furnifhed here*"
Of all thefe infcriptions, I am forry to obferve,

that

that " *Dealer in foreign fpirituous liquors*" is by
far the moft frequent   And indeed it is allowed by the Englifh themfelves, that the
propenfity of the common people to the
drinking of brandy or gin, is carried to a
great excefs   and I own it ftruck me as a
peculiar phrafeology, when, to tell you, that
a perfon is intoxicated or drunk, you hear
them fay, as they generally do, that *he is in
liquor*.   In the late riots, which even yet, are
hardly quite fubfided, and which are ftill the
general topic of converfation, more people
have been found dead near empty brandy-
cafks in the ftreets, than were killed by the
mufket balls of regiments, that were called
in.   As much as I have feen of London,
within thefe two days, there are on the whole
I think not very many very fine ftreets and
very fine houfes, but I met every where a far
greater number, and handfomer people, than
one commonly meets in Berlin   It gives me
much real pleafure, when I walk from Charing-crofs up the Strand, paft St. Paul's to
the Royal Exchange, to meet, in the thickeft
crowds, perfons, from the higheft to the loweft ranks, almoft all well-looking people and
cleanly and neatly dreffed.   I rarely fee even
a fel-

a fellow with a wheelbarrow, who has not a
fhirt on, and that too fuch an one, as fhews
it has been wafhed; nor even a beggar, without both a fhirt, and fhoes and ftockings.
The Englifh are certainly diftinguifhed for
cleanlinefs.

It has a very uncommon appearance in this
tumult of people, where every one, with hafty
and eager ftep, feems to be purfuing either
his bufinefs or his pleafure, and every where
making his way through the crowd, to obferve, as you often may, people pufhing, one
againft another, only perhaps to fee a funeral
pafs.   The Englifh coffins are made, very
œconomically, according to the exact form
of the body, they are flat, and broad at top;
tapering gradually from the middle, and
drawing to a point at the feet, not very unlike
the cafe of a violin.

A few dirty looking men, who bear the
coffin, endeavour to make their way through
the crowd, as well as they can; and fome
mourners follow.   The people feem to pay as
little attention to fuch a proceffion, as if a hay
cart were driving paft.   The funerals of people of diftinction and of the great, are however differently regarded.

Thefe

Thefe funerals always appear to me the more indecent in a populous city, from the total indifference of the beholders, and the perfect unconcern with which they are beheld.

The body of a fellow-creature is carried to his long home, as though it had been utterly unconnected with the reft of mankind. And yet, in a fmall town or village, every one knows every one: and no one can be fo infignificant, as not to be miffed, when he is taken away.

That fame influenza, which I left at Berlin, I have had the hard fortune again to find here; and many people die of it. It is as yet very cold for the time of the year, and I am obliged every day to have a fire. I muft own, that the heat or warmth given by fea-coal, burnt in the chimney, appears to me fofter, and milder, than that given by our ftoves. The fight of the fire has alfo a chearful and pleafing effect. Only you muft take care, not to look at it fteadily, and for a continuance, for this is probably the reafon that there are fo many young old-men in England, who walk and ride in the public ftreets, with their fpectacles on, thus anticipating,

C

in

in the bloom of youth, thofe conveniences and comforts, which were intended for old age.

I now conftantly dine in my own lodgings; and I cannot but flatter myfelf, that my meals are regulated with frugality.   My ufual difh at fupper is fome pickled falmon, which you eat in the liquor in which it is pickled, along with fome oil and vinegar; and he muft be prejudiced, or faftidious, who does not relifh it as fingularly well tafted and grateful food.

I would always advife thofe who wifh to drink coffee in England, to mention before hand how many cups are to be made with half an ounce; or elfe the people will probably bring them a prodigious quantity of brown water; which (notwithftanding all my ad-monitions) I have not yet been able wholly to avoid.   The fine wheaten bread which I find here,   befides   excellent   butter   and chefhire-cheefe,   makes   up   for   my   fcanty dinners.   For an Englifh dinner, to fuch lod-gers as I am,   generally confifts of a piece of half-boiled,   or half-roafted,   meat,   and a few cabbage leaves boiled   in   plain   water,   on which they pour a fauce made of flour and

butter.

butter. This, I assure you, is the usual method of dressing vegetables in England.

The slices of bread and butter, which they give you with your tea, are as thin as poppy leaves. But there is another kind of bread and butter usually eaten with tea, which is toasted by the fire, and is incomparably good. You take one slice after the other and hold it to the fire on a fork till the butter is melted, so that it penetrates a number of slices all at once this is called *Toast*.

The custom of sleeping without a feather-bed for a covering, particularly pleased me. You here lie between two sheets: underneath the bottom sheet is a fine blanket, which, without oppressing you, keeps you sufficiently warm. My shoes are not cleaned in the house, but by a person in the neighbourhood, whose trade it is, who fetches them every morning, and brings them back cleaned; for which she receives weekly so much. When the maid is displeased with me, I hear her sometimes at the door call me the *German*, otherwise in the family I go by the name of *the Gentleman*.

I have almost entirely laid aside riding in a coach, although it does not cost near so much

as

as it does at Berlin , as I can go and return
any diftance not exceeding an Englifh mile,
for a fhilling; for which I fhould there at
leaft pay a florin   But, moderate as Englifh
fares are, ftill you fave a great deal, if you
walk or go on foot , and know only how to
afk your way.   From my lodging to the
Royal Exchange, is about as far as from one
end of Berlin to the other , and from the
Tower and St. Catherine's, where the fhips
arrive in the Thames, as far again , and I
have already walked this diftance twice, when
I went to look after my trunk, before I got it
out of the fhip.   As it was quite dark, when
I came back the firft evening, I was aftonifhed at the admirable manner in which the
ftreets are lighted up; compared to which
our ftreets in Berlin make a moft miferable
fhew.   The lamps are lighted, whilft it is
ftill day-light , and are fo near each other,
that even on the moft ordinary and common
nights, the city has the appearance of a fef-
tive illumination , for which fome German
prince, who came to London for the firft
time, once, they fay, actually took it, and ferioufly believed it to have been particularly
ordered, on account of his arrival.

THE

THE 9*TH JUNE,* 1782.

I preached this day at the German church, on Ludgate-hill, for the Rev. Mr Wendeborn. He is the Author of " Der ſtatiſchen Bey-"trage zur nahern Kentniſs grofs Biittaniens." This valuable book has already been of un-common ſervice to me , and I cannot but re-commend it to every one, who goes to Eng-land.   It is the more uſeful, as you can with eaſe carry it in your pocket , and you find in it information on every ſubject.   It is natu-ral to ſuppoſe, that Mr. Wendeborn, who has now been a length of time in England, muſt have been able more ſiequently, and with greater exactneſs to make his obſerva-tions, than thoſe who only paſs through, or make a very ſhort ſtay.   It is almoſt impoſſi-ble for any one, who has this book always at hand, to omit any thing worthy of notice in or about London , or not to learn all that is moſt material to know, of the ſtate and ſitua-tion of the kingdom in general.

Mr. Wendeborn lives in New Inn, near Temple-bar, in a philoſophical, but not un-improving retirement.   He is almoſt become

C 3   a na-

a native; and his library confifts chiefly of
Englifh books.   Before I proceed, I muft juft
mention, that he has not hired, but bought
his apartments, in this great building, called
New Inn : and this, I believe, is pretty generally the cafe with the lodgings, in this place.
A purchafer of any of thefe rooms, is confidered as a proprietor, and one who has got
an houfe and home, and has a right in parliamentary, or other, elections, to give his vote,
if he is not a foreigner, which is the cafe with
Mr. Wendeborn, who, neverthelefs, was
vifited by Mr. Fox, when he was to be
chofen member for Weftminfter.

I faw, for the firft time, at Mr. Wendeborn's, a very ufeful machine, which is little
known in Germany, or at leaft not much
ufed.

This is a prefs in which, by means of very
ftrong iron fprings, a written paper may be
printed on another blank paper, and you thus
fave yourfelf the trouble of copying ; and at
the fame time multiply your own hand writing.   Mr. Werdeborn makes ufe of this
machine, every time he fends manufcripts
abroad, of which he wifhes to keep a copy.
This machine was of mahogany, and coft

pretty

pretty high. I fuppofe it is becaufe the inhabitants of London rife fo late, that divine
fervice begins only at half paft ten o'clock.
I miffed Mr. Wendeborn this morning, and
was therefore obliged to enquire of the door-
keeper at St. Paul's, for a direction to the
German church, where I was to preach.
He did not know it. I then afked at another
Church, not far from thence. Here I was
directed right, and after I had paffed through
an iron-gate to the end of a long paffage, I
arrived juft in time, at the church, where,
after the fermon, I was obliged to read a public
thankfgiving for the fafe arrival of our fhip.
The German clergy here, drefs exactly thefame
as the Englifh clergy, i e. in long robes with
wide fleeves, in which I likewife was obliged
to wrap myfelf Mr. Wendeborn wears
his own hair, which curls naturally, and the
toupee is combed up.

The other German clergymen, whom I
have feen, wear wigs, as well as many of the
Englifh.

I yefterday waited on our ambaffador,
Count Lucy, and was agreeably furprized at
the fimplicity of his manner of living. He
lives in a fmall private houfe. His fecretary

C 4 lives

lives up ſtairs, where alſo I met with the Pruſſian Conſul, who happened juſt then to be paying him a viſit.   Below, on the right hand, I was immediately ſhewn into his excellency's room, without being obliged to paſs through an anti-chamber. He wore a blue-coat with a red collar and red facings. He converſed with me, as we drank a diſh of coffee, on various learned topics, and when I told him of the great diſpute now going on about the taciſmus or ſtaciſmus, he declared himſelf, as a born Greek, for the *ſtaciſmus*. When I came to take my leave, he deſired me to come and ſee him without ceremony, whenever it ſuited me, as he ſhould be always happy to ſee me

Mr. Leonhard, who has tranſlated ſeveral celebrated Engliſh plays, ſuch as *The School for Scandal*, and ſome others, lives here as a private perſon, inſtructing Germans in Engliſh, and Engliſhmen in German, with great ability. He alſo it is, who writes the articles concerning England, for the new Hambro' newſpaper; for which he is paid a ſtated yearly ſtipend.   I may add alſo, that he is the maſter of a German freemaſon's lodge in London, and repreſentative of all the German lodges in England;

an

an employment of far more trouble, than pro-
fit, to him: for all the world applies to him in
all cafes and emergencies. I alfo was recommended to him from Hambro'. He is a
very complaifant man, and has already fhewn
me many civilities. He repeats Englifh
poetry with great propriety, and fpeaks the
language nearly with the fame facility as he
does his mother tongue. He is married to
an amiable Englifhwoman. I wifh him all
poffible happinefs. And now let me tell you
fomething of the fo often imitated, but perhaps inimitable

Vauxhall.

I yefterday vifited Vauxhall for the firft
time I had not far to go from my lodgings,
in the Adelphi-buildings, to Weftminfter-
Bridge, where you always find a great number of boats on the Thames, which are ready
on the leaft fignal to ferve thofe who will pay
them a fhilling or fixpence, according to the
diftance

From hence I went up the Thames to
Vauxhall, and as I paffed along, I faw Lam-
beth, and the venerable old palace belonging
to the archbifhops of Canterbury, lying on
my left.

Vauxhall is, properly fpeaking, the name of a little village in which the garden, now almoft exclufively bearing the fame name, is fituated. You pay a fhilling on entrance.

On entering it, I really found, or fancied I found, fome refemblance to our Berlin Vauxhall; if, according to Virgil, I may be permitted to compare fmall things with great ones. The walks at leaft, with the paintings at the end, and the high trees, which, here and there, form a beautiful grove, or wood, on either fide, were fo fimilar to thofe of Berlin, that often, as I walked along them, I feemed to tranfport myfelf, in imagination, once more to Berlin, and forgot for a moment, that immenfe feas and mountains, and kingdoms now lie between us. I was the more tempted to indulge in this reverie, as I actually met with feveral gentlemen, inhabitants of Berlin; in particular Mr. S***r, and fome others, with whom I fpent the evening in the moft agreeable manner. Here and there (particularly in one of the charming woods which art has formed in this garden) you are pleafingly furprized by the fudden appearance of the ftatues of the moft renowned Englifh poets and philofophers, fuch as Milton, Thom-

Thomſon, and others.   But, what gave me moſt pleaſure, was the ſtatue of the German compoſer, Handel, which, on entering the garden, is not far diſtant from the orcheſtra.

This orcheſtra is among a number of trees ſituated as in a little wood, and is an exceedingly handſome one.   As you enter the garden, you immediately hear the ſound of vocal and inſtrumental muſic.   There are ſeveral female ſingers conſtantly hired here to ſing in public.

On each ſide of the orcheſtra are ſmall boxes, with tables and benches, in which you ſup.   The walks before theſe, as well as in every other part of the garden, are crowded with people of all ranks.   I ſupped here with Mr. S* `r, and the ſecretary of the Pruſſian ambaſſador; beſides a few other gentlemen from Berlin, but what moſt aſtoniſhed me, was the boldneſs of the women of the town; who, along with their pimps, often ruſhed in upon us by half dozens, and in the moſt ſhameleſs manner importuned us for wine, for themſelves and their followers.   Our gentlemen thought it either unwiſe, unkind, or unſafe, to refuſe them ſo ſmall a boon altogether.

                                    An

An Englishman passed our box with hasty steps, and on our acquaintance's asking him, where he was going in such an hurry, he answered with an air of ridiculous importance, which set us all a laughing, " I have lost my girl !" He seemed to make his search, just as if he had been looking for a glove or a stick, which he had accidently dropt, or forgotten somewhere.

Lateish in the evening, we were entertained with a sight, that is indeed singularly curious and interesting. In a particular part of the garden, a curtain was drawn up, and by means of some mechanism, of extraordinary ingenuity, the eye and the ear are so completely deceived, that it is not easy to persuade one's-self it is a deception, and that one does not actually see and hear a natural waterfall from an high rock. As every one was flocking to this scene in crowds, there arose all at once, a loud cry of, " Take care of your pockets " This informed us, but too clearly, that there were some pick-pockets among the crowd, who had already made some fortunate strokes.

The rotunda, a magnificent circular building, in the garden, particularly engaged my attention. By means of beautiful chandeliers, and large mirrors, it was illuminated in the

moft

moſt ſupeib manner, and eveiy where deco-
rated with delightful paintings, and ſtatues,
in the contemplation of which you may ſpend
ſeveral hours very agreeably, when you are
tired of the crowd and the buſtle, in the
walks of the garden.

Among the paintings one repreſents the
ſurrender of a beſieged city. If you look at
this painting with attention, for any length of
time, it affeĉts you ſo much, that you even
ſhed tears. The expreſſion of the gieateſt
diſtreſs, even bordeing on deſpair, on the
part of the beſieged, the fearful expeĉtation of
the uncertain iſſue, and what the viĉtor will
deteimine concerning thoſe unfortunate people, may all be read ſo plainly, and ſo natu-
ially in the countenances of the inhabitants
who are imploring for mercy, from the hoaiy
head to the ſuckling whom his mothcr holds
up, that you quite forget yourſelf, and in the
end ſcarcely believe it to be a painting before you.

You alſo here find the buſts of the beſt
Engliſh authors, placed all round on the ſides.
Thus a Briton again meets with his Shake-
ſpear, Locke, Milton, and Diyden, in the
public places of his amuſements; and there
alſo

alfo reveres their memory. Even the common people thus become familiar with the names of thofe who have done honour to their nation; and are taught to mention them with veneration   For this rotunda is alfo an orcheftra, in which the mufic is performed, in rainy weather.   But enough of Vauxhall !

Certain it is, that the Englifh claffical authors are read more generally, beyond all comparifon than the German , which in general are read only by the learned, or, at moft, by the middle clafs of people.   The Englifh national authors are in all hands, and read by all people, of which the innumerable editions they have gone through, are a fufficient proof.

My landlady, who is only a taylor's widow, reads her Milton, and tells me, that her late hufband firft fell in love with her, on this very account , becaufe fhe read Milton with fuch proper emphafis.   This fingle inftance perhaps would prove but little , but I have converfed with feveral people of the lower clafs, who all knew their national authors, and who all have read many, if not all of them.   This elevates the lower ranks, and brings them nearer to the higher.   There is hardly any

ar-

argument, or dispute in conversation, in the higher ranks, about which the lower cannot also converse or give their opinion. Now in Germany, since Gellest, there has as yet been no poet's name familiar to the people. But the quick sale of the classical authors, is here promoted also, by cheap and convenient editions. They have them all bound in pocket volumes, as well as in a more pompous stile. I myself bought Milton in duodecimo for two shillings, neatly bound, it is such an one as I can, with great convenience, carry in my pocket. It also appears to me to be a good fashion, which prevails here, and here only, that the books which are most read, are always to be had, already well and neatly bound. At stalls, and in the streets, you every now and then meet with a sort of antiquarians, who sell single or odd volumes, sometimes perhaps of Shakespear, &c. so low as a penny, nay even sometimes for an halfpenny a piece. Of one of these itinerant antiquarians I bought the two volumes of the Vicar of Wakefield, for sixpence, *i. e.* for the half of an English shilling. In what estimation our German literature is held in England, I was enabled to judge, in some degree, by the printed

pro-

propofals of a book, which I faw. The title
was "The Entertaining Mufeum, or Complete Circulating Library," which is to contain
a lift of all the Englifh claffical authors, as
well as tranflations of the beft French, Spa-
nifh, Italian, and *even German novels*.

The moderate price of this book deferves
alfo to be noticed, as by fuch means books
in England come more within the reach of
the people; and of courfe are more generally
diftributed among them. The advertifement
mentions, that in order that every one may
have it in his power to buy this work and at
once to furnifh himfelf with a very valuable
library, without perceiving the expence, a
number will be fent out weekly, which, ftitch-
ed, cofts fixpence, and bound with the title
on the back, nine-pence. The twenty-fifth
and twenty-fixth number, contain the firft
and fecond volume of the vicar of Wakefield,
which I had juft bought of the antiquarian
above mentioned.

The only tranflation from the German
which has been particularly fuccefsful in England, is " Gefner's Death of Abel." The
tranflation of that work has been oftener re-
printed in England, than ever the original

was

was in Germany. I have actually feen the eighteenth edition of it : and if the Englifh preface is to be regarded, it was written by a lady. " Klopftock's Meffiah," as is well known has been here but ill received. to be fure, they fay, it is but indiffeiently tranflated. I have not yet been able to obtain a fight of it. The Rev. Mr Wendeboin has written a grammar for the German language in Englifh, for the ufe of Englifhmen, which has met with much applaufe. I muft not forget to mention that the works of Mr Jacob Boehmen, are all tianflated into Englifh.

LONDON, 13TH JUNE.

OFTEN as I had heard Ranelagh spoken of, I had yet formed only an imperfect idea of it. I supposed it to be a garden some-what different from that of Vauxhall; but, in fact, I hardly knew what I thought of it. Yesterday evening I took a walk, in order to visit this famous place of amusement; but I missed my way and got to Chelsea; where I met a man with a wheelbarrow, who not only very civilly shewed me the right road, but also conversed with me the whole of the distance, which we walked together. And finding, on enquiry, that I was a subject of the King of Prussia, he desired me, with much eagerness, to relate to him some anecdotes concerning that mighty monarch.

At length I arrived at Ranelagh; and having paid my half-crown, on entrance, I soon enquired for the garden door, and it was readily shewn to me; when, to my infinite astonishment, I found myself in a poor, mean-looking, and ill-lighted garden, where I met but few people. I had not been here long before I was accosted by a young lady, who

alfo

also was walking there, and who, without ceremony, offered me her arm, asking me why I walked thus solitarily? I now concluded, this could not possibly be the splendid, much-boasted Ranelagh, and so, seeing not far from me a number of people entering a door, I followed them, in hopes either to get out again, or to vary the scene.

But it is impossible to describe, or indeed to conceive, the effect it had on me, when, coming out of the gloom of the garden, I suddenly entered a round building, illuminated by many hundred lamps, the splendor and beauty of which surpassed every thing of the kind I had ever seen before. Every thing seemed here, to be round: above, there was a gallery, divided into boxes, and in one part of it an organ with a beautiful choir, from which issued both instrumental and vocal music. All around, under this gallery, are handsome painted boxes for those who wish to take refreshments: the floor was covered with mats, in the middle of which are four high black pillars, within which there are neat fire places for preparing tea, coffee, and punch: and all around also there are placed tables, set out with all kinds of refreshments. Within
these

thefe four pillars, in a kind of magic rotundo, all the beau-monde of London move perpetually round and round.

I at firft mixed with this immenfe concourfe of people, of all fexes, ages, countries, and characters: and I muft confefs, that the inceffant change of faces, the far greater number of which were ftrikingly beautiful, together with the illumination, the extent and majeftic fplendor of the place, with the continued found of the mufic, makes an inconceivably delightful impreffion on the imagination, and I take the liberty to add, that, on feeing it now for the firft time, I felt pretty nearly the fame fenfations, that I remember to have felt, when, in early youth, I firft read the Fairy Tales.

Being however at length tired of the crowd, and being tired alfo, with always moving round and round in a circle, I fat myfelf down in one of the boxes, in order to take fome refrefhment, and was now contemplating at my eafe, this prodigious collection and crowd of an happy, cheaiful world, who were here enjoying themfelves devoid of care, when a waiter very civilly afked me what refrefhment I wifhed to have, and in a

few

few moments returned with what I asked for. To my astonishment, he would accept no money for these refreshments; which I could not comprehend, till he told me that every thing was included in the half-crown I had paid at the door; and that I had only to command, if I wished for any thing more, but that, if I pleased, I might give him as a present a trifling douceur. This I gave him with pleasure, as I could not help fancying, I was hardly entitled to so much civility and good attendance for one single half-crown.

I now went up into the gallery, and seated myself in one of the boxes there : and from thence becoming, all at once, a grave and moralizing spectator, I looked down on the concourse of people, who were still moving round and round in the fairy circle; and then I could easily distinguish several stars, and other orders, of knighthood, French queues and bags contrasted with plain English heads of hair, or professional wigs, old age and youth, nobility and commonalty, all passing each other in the motley swarm. An Englishman who joined me, during this my reverie, pointed out to me on my enquiring, princes, and lords with their dazzling stars, with which they

they eclipſed the leſs brilliant part of the company.

Here ſome moved round in an eternal circle to ſee and be ſeen, there a groupe of eager connoiſſeurs had placed themſelves before the orcheſtra and were feaſting their ears, while others, at the well ſupplied tables, were regaling the parched roofs of their mouths, in a more ſubſtantial manner, and again others like myſelf were ſitting alone, in the corner of a box in the gallery, making their remarks and reflexions on ſo intereſting a ſcene.

I now and then indulged myſelf in the pleaſure of exchanging, for ſome minutes, all this magnificence and ſplendor, for the gloom of the garden, in order to renew the pleaſing ſurprize I experienced on my firſt entering the building. Thus I ſpent here ſome hours in the night, in a continual variation of entertainment, when the crowd now all at once began to leſſen, and I alſo took a coach and drove home

At Ranelagh, the company appeared to me much better, and more ſelect than at Vauxhall, for thoſe of the lower claſs, who go there, always dreſs themſelves in their beſt; and thus endeavour to copy the great. Here
I ſaw

I saw no one who had not silk stockings on.
Even the poorest families are at the expence
of a coach, to go to Ranelagh, as my landlady
assured me.   She always fixed on some one
day in the year, on which, without fail, she
drove to Ranelagh.   On the whole the expence at Ranelagh is nothing near so great as
it is at Vauxhall, if you consider the refreshments, for any one who sups at Vauxhall,
which most people do, is likely for a very
moderate supper, to pay at least half-a-
guinea.

The Parliament.

I had almost forgotten to tell you, that I
have already been to the Parliament House:
and yet this is of most importance.   For,
had I seen nothing else in England, but this,
I should have thought my journey thither
amply rewarded.

As little as I have hitherto troubled myself
with politics, because indeed with us, it is
but little worth our while, I was however de-
sirous to be present at a meeting of parliament, a wish that was soon amply gratified.

One afternoon about three o'clock, at
which hour, or thereabouts, the house most

commonly meets, I enquired for Weftminfter-Hall, and was very politely directed by an Englifhman. Thefe directions are always given with the utmoft kindnefs. You may afk whom you pleafe if you can only make yourfelf tolerably well underftood, and by thus afking, every now and then, you may with the greateft eafe find your way throughout all London.

Weftminfter-Hall is an enormous gothic building, whofe vaulted roof is fuppoited not by pillars, but inftead of thefe there are on each fide, large unnatural heads of angels, carved in wood, which feem to fupport the roof.

When you have paffed through this long hall, you afcend a few fteps at the end, and are led through a daik paffage into the Houfe of Commons, which, below, has a large double dooi, and above, there is a fmall ftaii-cafe, by which you go to the gallery, the place allotted for ftrangeis.

The firft time I went up this fmall ftair-cafe and had reached the rails, I faw a veiy genteel man in black, ftanding there. I ac-cofted him, without any intioduction, and I afked him whether I might be allowed to go into the gallery. He told me, that I muſt be introduced by a member, or elſe I could not get admiſſion there. Now as I had not the honour to be acquainted with a member, I was under the mortifying neceſſity of re-treating, and again going down ſtairs, as I did, much chagrined. And now, as I was ſullenly marching back, I heard ſomething ſaid about a bottle of wine, which ſeemed to be addreſſed to me. I could not conceive what it could mean, till I got home, when my obliging landlady told me, I ſhould have given the well-dreſſed man, half-a-crown, or a couple of ſhillings, for a bottle of wine. Happy in this information, I went again the next day, when the ſame man, who before had ſent me away, after I had given him only two ſhillings, very politely opened the door for me, and himſelf recommended me to a good ſeat in the gallery.

And thus I now, for the firſt time, ſaw the whole of the Britiſh nation aſſembled in its repreſentatives, in rather a mean-looking building, that not a little reſembles a chapel. The Speaker, an elderly man, with an enor-mous wig, with two knotted kind of treſſes, or curls, behind, in a black cloak, his hat on

D   his

his head, fat oppofite to me on a lofty chair, which was not unlike a fmall pulpit, fave only that in the front of this there was no reading defk. Before the Speaker's chair ftands a table, which looks like an altar, and at this there fit two men, called clerks, dreffed in black, with black cloaks. On the table, by the fide of the great parchment acts, lies an huge gilt fceptre, which is always taken away and placed in a confervatory under the table, as foon as ever the Speaker quits the chair; which he does as often as the houfe refolves itfelf into a committee A committee means nothing more than that the houfe puts itfelf into a fituation freely to difcufs and debate any point of difficulty and moment, and, while it lafts, the Speaker partly lays afide his power as a legiflator. As foon as this is over, fome one tells the Speaker, that he may now again be feated! and immediately on the Speaker's being again in the chair the fceptre is alfo re-placed on the table before him.

All round on the fides of the houfe under the gallery, are benches for the members, co-vered with green cloth, always one above the other, like our choirs in churches, in order that he who is fpeaking, may fee over thofe
who

who fit before him. The feats in the gallery are on the fame plan. The Members of Parliament keep their hats on, but the fpectatois in the gallery are uncovered.

The Members of the Houfe of Commons have nothing particular in their drefs, they even come into the houfe, in their great coats, and with boots and fpurs. It is not at all uncommon to fee a member lying ftietched out on one of the benches, while others are debating. Some crack nuts, otheis eat oranges, or whatever elfe is in feafon. There is no end to their going in and out; and as often as any one wifhes to go out, he places himfelf befoie the fpeaker, and makes him his bow, as if like a fchool-boy, he afked his tutor's permiffion.

Thofe who fpeak, feem to deliver themfelves with but little, perhaps not always with even a decorous, gravity. All that is neceffary, is to ftand up in your place, take off your hat, turn to the Speaker, (to whom all the fpeeches aie addieffed,) to hold your hat and ftick in one hand, and with the other hand to make any fuch motions as you fancy neceffary to accompany your fpeech.

If

If it happens, that a member rifes, who is but a bad fpeaker; or if what he fays is geneially deemed not fufficiently interefling, fo much noife is made, and fuch buifls of laughter are raifed, that the member who is fpeaking can fcaicely diftinguifh his own woids. This muft needs be a diftieffing fituation; and it feems then to be paiticulaily laughable, when the Speaker in his chair, like a tutor in a fchool, again and again endeavouis to reftore order, which he does by calling out *to order, to order*, apparently often without much attention being paid to it.

On the contiary, when a favouiite member, and one who fpeaks well and to the purpofe, iifes, the moft perfect filence reigns: and his friends and admirers, one after anothei, make their approbation known by calling out, *hear him*, which is often repeated by the whole houfe at once; and in this way fo much noife is often made that the Speaker is fiequently interrupted by this fame emphatic *hear him*. Notwithftanding which, this calling out is always regarded as a great encouragement, and I have often obferved, that one who began with fome diffidence, and

even

even fomewhat inaufpicioufly, has in the end
been fo animated, that he has fpoken with a
torrent of eloquence.

As all fpeeches are directed to the Speaker,
all the members always preface their fpeeches
with, *fir*, and he, on being thus addreffed,
generally moves his hat a little, but immediately puts it on again. This *fir* is often introduced in the courfe of their fpeeches, and
ferves to connect what is faid . it feems alfo
to ftand the fpeaker in fome ftead, when any
one's memory fails him, or he is otherwife
at a lofs for matter. For while he is faying,
fir, and has thus obtained a little paufe, he
recollects what is to follow. Yet I have fometimes feen fome members draw a kind of memorandum out of their pockets, like a can-
didate who is at a lofs in his fermon this
is the only inftance in which a member of
the Britifh parliament feems to read his
fpeeches.

The firft day that I was at the Houfe of
Commons, an Englifh gentleman, who fat
next to me in the gallery, very obligingly
pointed out to me the principal members;
fuch as *Fox*, *Burke*, *Rigby*, &c all of whom
I heard fpeak. The debate happened to be

whether,

whether, befides being made a peer, any
other fpecific reward fhould be beftowed by
the nation on their gallant admiral Rodney.
In the courfe of the debate, I remember,
Mr. Fox was very fharply reprimanded by
young Lord Fielding, for having, when minifter, oppofed the election of Admiral Hood,
as a member for Weftminfter.

Fox was fitting to the right of the Speaker,
not far from the table on which the gilt
fceptre lay.   He now took his place fo near
it that he could reach it with his hand, and,
thus placed, he gave it many a violent and
hearty thump, either to aid, or to fhew, the
energy with which he fpoke.   If the charge
was vehement, his defence was no lefs fo:
he juftified himfelf againft Lord Fielding, by
maintaining, that he had not oppofed this
election in the character of a minifter, but as
an individual, or private perfon   and that, as
fuch, he had freely and honeftly given his
vote for another, namely for Sir Cecil Wray;
adding, that the King when he appointed him
fecretary of ftate, had entered into no agree-
ment with him, by which he loft his vote
as an individual. to fuch a requifition he
never would have fubmitted. It is impoffible

for me to defcribe, with what fire, and
perfuafive eloquence he fpoke, and how the
Speaker in the chair inceffantly nodded approbation from beneath his folemn wig, and
innumerable voices inceffantly called out,
hear him! hear him! and when there was the
leaft fign that he intended to leave off fpeaking, they no lefs vociferoufly exclaimed, *go
on*, and fo he continued to fpeak in this
manner for nearly two hours. Mr. Rigby
in reply, made a fhort but humourous fpeech,
in which he mentioned of how little confequence the title of *lord* and *lady* was without
money to fupport it, and finifhed with the
latin proverb, " infelix paupertas,—quia ri-
" diculos miferos facit." After having firft
very judicioufly obferved, that previous enquiry fhould be made, whether Admiral Rodney had made any rich prizes or captures;
becaufe, if that fhould be the cafe, he would
not ftand in need of further reward in money.
I have fince been almoft every day at the
parliament houfe, and prefer the entertainment I there meet with, to moft other amufe-
ments.

Fox is ftill much beloved by the people,
notwithftanding that they are, (and certainly

with

with good reafon) difpleafed at his being the
caufe of Admiral Rodney's recall, though
even I have heard him again and again,
almoft extravagant in his encomiums on this
noble admiral. This fame celebrated Charles
Fox is a fhort, fat, and grofs, man, with a
fwarthy complexion, and dark, and in general
he is badly dreffed. There certainly is fomething Jewifh in his looks. But upon the whole,
he is not an ill made nor an ill looking man :
and there are many ftrong marks of fagacity
and fire in his eyes. I have frequently heard
the people here fay, that this fame Mr. Fox
is as cunning as a Fox. Burke is a well-made,
tall, upright man, but looks elderly and
broken. Rigby is exceffively corpulent, and
has a jolly rubicund face.

The little lefs than downright open abufe,
and the many really rude things, which the
members faid to each other, ftruck me much.
For example, when one has finifhed, another
rifes, and immediately taxes with abfurdity
all that *the right honourable gentleman*, (for with
this title the members of the Houfe of Commons always honour each other) had juft advanced. It would indeed be contrary to the
rules of the houfe, flatly to tell each other,

that

that what they have spoken, is *false*, or even *foolish*: instead of this, they turn themselves, as usual, to the Speaker, and so, whilst their address is directed to him, they fancy they violate neither the rules of parliament, nor those of good breeding and decorum, whilst they utter the most cutting personal sarcasms against the member, or the measure they oppose.

It is quite laughable to see, as one sometimes does, one member speaking, and another accompanying the speech with his action. This I remarked more than once in a worthy old citizen, who was fearful of speaking himself, but when his neighbour spoke, he accompanied every energetic sentence with a suitable gesticulation, by which means, his whole body was sometimes in motion

It often happens that the jett, or principal point, in the debate, is lost in these personal contests, and bickerings between each other. When they last so long as to become quite tedious and tiresome, and likely to do harm rather than good, the house takes upon itself to express its disapprobation; and then there arises a general cry, of *the question ! the question !* This must sometimes be frequently repeated, as the contending members are both anxious

to.

to have the laſt word. At length however
the queſtion is put, and the votes taken;
when the Speaker ſays: " thoſe who are for
" the queſtion, are to ſay *aye*, and thoſe who
" are againſt it, *no!*" You then hear a con-
fuſed cry of *aye* and *no:* but, at length, the
Speaker ſays: " I think there are more *ayes*
" than *noes*, or more *noes* than *ayes*. The
" *ayes* have it; or the *noes* have it," as the
caſe may be. But all the ſpectators muſt then
retire from the gallery: for then, and not till
then, the voting really commences. And
now the members call aloud to the gallery,
withdraw! withdraw! On this the ſtrangers
withdraw, and are ſhut up in a ſmall room, at
the foot of the ſtairs till the voting is over,
when they are again permitted to take their
places in the gallery. Here I could not help
wondering at the impatience even of poliſhed
Engliſhmen; it is aſtoniſhing with what vio-
lence, and even rudeneſs, they puſh and joſtle
one another, as ſoon as the room door is again
opened, eager to gain the firſt and beſt
ſeats in the gallery. In this manner we, the
ſtrangers, have ſometimes been ſent away two
or three times, in the courſe of one day, or
rather evening, afterwards again permitted

to

to return. Among these spectators are people of all ranks, and even, not unfrequently, ladies. Two short-hand writers have sat sometimes not far distant from me, who, (though it is rather by stealth) endeavour to take down, the words of the speaker, and thus all that is very remarkable in what is said in parliament, may generally be read *in print,* the next day. The short-hand writers, whom I noticed, are supposed to be employed and paid by the editors of the different newspapers. There are it seems some few persons who are constant attendants on the parliament, and so they pay the door-keeper beforehand a guinea for a whole session. I have now and then seen some of the members bring their sons, whilst quite little boys, and carry them to their seats along with themselves.

A proposal was once made to erect a gallery in the house of peers also, for the accomodation of spectators. But this never was carried into effect. There appears to be much more politeness and more courteous behaviour in the members of the upper house. But he who wishes to observe mankind, and to contemplate the leading traits of the different characters, most strongly marked, will do

D 6 well

well to attend frequently the lower, rather than the other, houfe.

Laft Tuefday was (what is here called) *hanging day.* There was alfo a parliamentary election: I *could* only fee *one* of the two fights; and therefore naturally preferred the latter, while I only heard tolling at a diftance the death-bell of the facrifice to juftice. I now therefore am going to defcribe to you, as well as I can, an

Election for a Member of Parliament.

The cities of London and Weftminfter fend, the one four, and the other two members to parliament. Mr. Fox is one of the two members for Weftminfter, one feat was vacant, and that vacancy was now to be filled And the fame Sir Cecil Wray, whom Fox had before oppofed to Lord Hood, was now publicly chofen. They tell me, that at thefe elections when there is a ftrong oppofition-party, there is often bloody work, but this election was, in the electioneering phrafe, an *hollow thing,* i. e. quite fure, as thofe who had voted for Admiral Hood now withdrew, without ftanding a poll; as being convinced beforehand, their chance to fucceed was defperate.

I

The

The election was held in Covent-Garden, a large market-place, in the open air. There was a scaffold erected just before the door of a very handsome church, which also is called *St Paul's*, but which however is not to be compared to the cathedral.

A temporary edifice, formed only of boards and wood nailed together, was erected on the occasion. It was called *the hustings* : and filled with benches, and at one end of it, where the benches ended, mats were laid, on which those, who spoke to the people, stood. In the area before the hustings, immense multitudes of people were assembled, of whom the greatest part seemed to be of the lowest order. To this tumultuous crowd, however, the speakers often bowed very low, and always addressed them by the title of *gentlemen*. Sir Cecil Wray was obliged to step forward and promise these same *gentlemen*, with hand and heart, that he would faithfully fulfil his duties, as their representative. He also made an apology, because, on account of his journey and ill-health, he had not been able to wait on them, as became him, at their respective houses. The moment that he began to speak even this rude rabble became all as quiet as
the

the raging fea after a ftorm ; only every now and then rending the air with the parliamentary cry of *hear him! hear him!* and as foon as he had done fpeaking, they again vociferated a loud and univerfal huzza, every one at the fame time waving his hat.

And now, being formally declared to have been legally chofen, he again bowed moft profoundly, and returned thanks for the great honour done him : when a well-dreffed man, whofe name I could not learn, ftepped forward, and in a well indited fpeech congratulated both the chofen and the chufers. " Upon my word," faid a gruff carter, who ftood near me, " that man fpeaks well."

Even little boys clambered up and hung on the rails and on the lamp-pofts ; and as if the fpeeches had alfo been addreffed to them, they too liftened with the utmoft attention : and they too teftified their approbation of it, by joining luftily in the three cheers, and waving their hats.

All the enthufiafm of my earlieft years, kindled by the patriotifm of the illuftrious heroes of Rome, Coriolanus, Julius Cæfar, and Antony, were now revived in my mind : and though all I had juft feen and heard, be, in fact, but the femblance of liberty, and that too tribunitial liberty, yet at that moment, I thought it charming, and it warmed my heart. Yes, depend on it, my friend, when you here fee how in this happy country, the loweft and meaneft member of fociety, thus unequivocally teftifies the intereft which he takes in every thing of a public nature, when you fee, how even women and children bear a part in the great concerns of their country; in fhort, how high and low, rich, and poor, all concur in declaring their feelings and their convictions, that a carter, a common tar, or a fcavenger, is ftill a man, nay, an Englifh-man; and as fuch has his rights and privi-leges defined and known as exactly and as well as his king, or as his king's minifter—take my word for it, you will feel yourfelf very differently affected from what you are, when ftaring at our foldiers in their exercifes at Berlin.

When Fox, who was among the voters, arrived at the beginning of the election, he too was received with an univerfal fhout of joy. At length when it was nearly over, the people took it into their heads to hear him fpeak, and every one called out *Fox! Fox!* I

know

know not why, but I feemed to catch fome
of the fpirit of the place and time, and fo I
alfo bawled, *Fox, Fox!* and he was obliged to
come forward and fpeak: for no other reafon
that I could find, but that the people wifhed
to hear him fpeak   In this fpeech, he again
confirmed, in the prefence of the people, his
former declaration in parliament, that he by
no means had any influence as minifter of
ftate in this election, but only and merely as a
private perfon.

When the whole was over, the rampant
fpirit of liberty, and the wild impatience of a
genuine Englifh mob were exhibited in perfection.   In a very few minutes the whole
fcaffolding, benches, and chairs, and every
thing elfe, was completely deftroyed, and
the mat with which it had been covered torn
into ten thoufand long ftrips or pieces, or
ftrings; with which they *encircled* or enclofed
multitudes of people of all ranks.   Thefe
they hurried along with them and every thing
elfe that came in their way, as trophies of
joy. and thus, in the midft of exultation and
triumph, they paraded through many of the
moft populous ftreets of London.

Whilft

Whilst in Pruffia, poets only fpeak of the love of country, as one of the deareft of all human affections, here, there is no man who does not feel, and defcribe with rapture how much he loves his country. "Yes, for my "country I'll fhed the laft drop of my "blood!" often exclaims little Jacky, the fine boy here in the houfe where I live, who is yet only about twelve years old. The love of their country and its unparalleled feats in war, are, in general, the fubject of their ballads and popular fongs, which are fung about the ftreets by women, who fell them for a few farthings. It was only the other day our *Jacky* brought one home, in which the hiftory of an admiral was celebrated, who bravely continued to command, even after his two legs were fhot off, and he was obliged to be fupported. I know not well by what means it has happened, that the king of England, who is certainly one of the beft the nation ever had, is become unpopular. I know not how many times I have heard people of all forts object to their king, at the fame time that they praifed the king of Pruffia to the fkies. Indeed, with fome, the veneration for our monarch went fo far, that

they

they ferioufly wifhed he was their king All that feems to fhock and difhearten them is the pro-digious armies he keeps up , and the immenfe number of foldiers quartered in Berlin alone. Whereas in London, at leaft in the city, not a fingle troop of foldiers of the king's guard, dare make their appearance.

A few days ago, I faw (what is here deemed a great fight) viz. a lord-mayor's proceffion. The lord-mayor was in an enormous large gilt coach, which was followed by an aftonifhing number of moft fhewy carriages, in which the reft of the city-magiftrates, more properly called aldermen of London, were feated. But enough for the prefent.

LONDON, JUNE 17TH, 1782.

I HAVE now been pretty nearly all over London, and, according to my own notions, have now seen moſt of the things I was moſt anxious to ſee. Hereafter then, I propoſe to make an excurſion into the country, and this purpoſe, by the bleſſing of God, I hope to be able to carry into effect in a very few days, for, my curioſity is here almoſt ſatiated, I ſeem to be tired and ſick of the ſmoke of theſe ſea-coal fires, and I long, with almoſt childiſh impatience, once more, to breathe a freſher and clearer air.

It muſt, I think, be owned, that upon the whole, London is neither ſo handſomely nor ſo well built as Berlin is, but then it certainly has far more fine ſquares. Of theſe there are many that in real magnificence, and beautiful ſymmetry, far ſurpaſs our *Gens d'Armes Markt,* our *Denhoſchen,* and *Williams Place.* Theſe ſquares, or quadrangular places, contain the beſt and moſt beautiful buildings of London. a ſpacious ſtreet, next to the houſes, goes all round them, and within that there is generally a round graſs-plot, railed in with

iron rails, in the centre of which, in many of
of them, there is a ftatue, which ftatues moft
commonly are equeftrian and gilt.   In
Grofvenor-fquare, inftead of this green plot,
or area, there is a little circular wood, intended, no doubt, to give one the idea of
rus in urbe.

One of the longeft and pleafanteft walks
I have yet taken is from Paddington to
Iflington, where to the left you have a fine
profpect of the neighbouring hills, and in
particular of the village of Hampftead, which
is built on one of them ; and to the right the
ftreets of London furnifh an endlefs variety of
interefting views.   It is true, that it is dangerous to walk here alone, efpecially in the
afternoon, and in an evening, or at night, for it
was only laft week that a man was robbed and
murdered on this very fame road.   But I now
haften to another and a more pleafing topic :

The Britifh Mufeum.

I have had the happinefs to become acquainted with the Rev. Mr. Woide ; who,
though well known, all over Europe, to be
one of the moft learned men of the age, is yet,
if poffible, lefs eftimable for his learning,
than

than he is for his unaffected goodnefs of heart. He holds a refpectable office in the Mufeum, and was obliging enough to procure me permiffion to fee it, luckily the day before it was fhut up. In general you muft give in your name a fortnight before you can be admitted. But, after all, I am forry to fay, it was the rooms, the glafs cafes, the fhelves, or the repofitory for the books in the Britifh Mufeum which I faw, and not the Mufeum itfelf, we were hurried on fo rapidly through the apartments. The company, who faw it when and as I did, was various, and fome of all forts; fome, I believe, of the very loweft claffes of the people, of both fexes, for, as it is the property of the nation, every one has the fame right (I ufe the term of the country) to fee it, that another has. I had Mr Wendeborn's book in my pocket, and it, at leaft, enabled me to take a fomewhat more particular notice of fome of the principal things, fuch as the Egyptian mummy, an head of Homer, &c. The reft of the company obferving that I had fome affiftance, which they had not, foon gathered round me; I pointed out to them, as we went along, from Mr. Wendeborn's German book, what

what there was moft worth feeing here.   The
gentleman, who conducted us, took little pains
to conceal the contempt which he felt for my
communications, when he found out that it was
only a German defcription of the Britifh Mu-
fuem I had got.   The rapidly paffing through
this vaft fuite of rooms, in a fpace of time,
little, if at all, exceeding an hour, with leifure
juft to caft one poor longing look of aftonifhment on all thefe ftupenduous treafures of
natural curiofities, antiquities, and literature;
in the contemplation of which you could with
pleafure fpend years, and a whole life might
be employed in the ftudy of them—quite con-
fufes, ftuns, and overpowers one.   In fome
branches this collection is faid to be far furpaffed by fome others; but taken all together,
and for fize, it certainly is equalled by none.
The few foreign divines, who travel through
England, generally defire to have the Alexandrian manufcript fhewn them, in order to
be convinced, with their own eyes, whether
the paffage, " Thefe are the three that bear
" record, &c." is to be found there or not.

    The Rev Mr. Woide lives at a place called
Liffon-ftreet, not far from Paddington, a
very village-looking little town, at the weft

end of London. It is quite a rural and pleafant fituation, for here, I either do, or fancy I do, already breathe a purer and freer air than in the midft of the town. Of his great abilities, and particularly in oriental literature, I need not inform you, but it will give you pleafure to hear that he is actually meditating a fac-fimile edition of the Alexandrian M. S. I have already mentioned the infinite obligations I lie under to this excellent man for his extraordinary courtefy and kindnefs.

The Theatre in the Hay-market.

Laft week I went twice to an Englifh play-houfe. The firft time *The Nabob* was reprefented, of which the late Mr. Foot was the author, and for the entertainment, a very pleafing and laughable mufical farce, called *The Agreeable Surprize*, the fecond time I faw *The Englifh Merchant*; which piece has been tranflated into German, and is known among us by the title of *The Scotchwoman*, or, *The Coffee-houfe*. I have not yet feen the theatres at Covent-garden and Drury-lane, becaufe they are not open in fummer. The beft actors alfo, ufually fpend May and October in the country, and only perform in winter.

A very

A very few excepted, the comedians whom I saw, were certainly nothing extraordinary. For a feat in the boxes you pay five shillings, in the pit thrice, in the first gallery two, and in the second, or upper gallery, one shilling. And it is the tenants in this upper gallery who, for their shilling, make all that noise and uproar, for which the English play-houses are so famous. I was in the pit, which gradually rises, amphi-theatre-wise, from the orcheftra, and is furnished with benches, one above another from the top to the bottom. Often, and often whilst I sat here, did a rotten orange, or pieces of the peel of an orange, fly past me, or past some of my neighbours, and once one of them actually hit my hat, without my daring to look round, for fear another might then hit me on my face.

All over London, as one walks, one every where, in the season, sees oranges to sell, and they are in general, sold tolerably cheap, one and even sometimes two for a halfpenny; or, in our money, three-pence. At the play-house, however, they charged me six-pence for one orange, and that no ways remarkably good.

Besides this perpetual pelting from the gallery, which renders an English play-house so
uncomfortable,

uncomfortable, their is no end to their calling out and knocking with their flicks, till the curtain, is drawn up. I faw a miller's, or a baker's boy, thus like a huge booby, leaning over the rails and knocking, again and again, on the outfide, with all his might, fo that he was feen by every body, without being in the leaft afhamed or abafhed. I fometimes heard too the people in the lower or middle gallery quarrelling with thofe of the upper one. Behind me, in the pit, fat a young fop who, in order to difplay his coftly ftone-buckles with the utmoft brilliancy, continually put his foot on my bench, and even fometimes upon my coat, which I could avoid only by fparing him as much fpace, from my portion of the feat, as would make him a foot-ftool.

In the boxes, quite in a corner, fat feveral fervants, who were faid to be placed there, to keep the feats for the families they ferved, till they fhould arrive, they feemed to fit remarkably clofe and ftill, the reafon of which, I was told, was their apprehenfion of being pelted, for, if one of them dares but to look out of the box, he is immediately faluted with a fhower of orange peel from the gallery.

E   In

In Foot's *Nabob* there are fundry local
and perfonal fatires, which are entirely loft to
a foreigner. The character of the *Nabob* was
performed by a Mr. Palmer. The jett of the
character is, this Nabob with many affected
airs, and conftant aims at gentility, is ftill but
a filly fellow, unexpectedly come into the
poffeffion of immenfe riches, and therefore,
of courfe, paid much court to by a fociety of
natural philofophers, quakers, and I do not
know who befides. Being tempted to become one of their members, he is elected;
and in order to ridicule thefe would-be philofophers, but real knaves, a fine flowery
fuftian fpeech is put into his mouth, which he
delivers with prodigious pomp and importance, and is liftened to by the philofophers
with infinite complacency. The two fcenes
of the quakers and philofophers, who with
countenances full of imaginary importance
were feated at a green table, with their pre-
fident at their head, while the fecretary with
the utmoft care was making an inventory of
the ridiculous prefents of the *Nabob*, were
truly laughable. One of the laft fcenes was
beft received. It is that, in which the Nabob's friend and fchoolfellow vifit him, and
                                    addrefs

addrefs him without ceremony, by his Chriftian name, but to all their queftions of " Whether he does not recollect them?" " Whether he does remember fuch and fuch " a play? or fuch and fuch a fcrape, into " which they had fallen in their youth?" He uniformly anfwers with a look of ineffable contempt, only, " *No Sir*!" Nothing can poffibly be more ludicrous, nor more comic.

The entertainment, *The Agreeable Surprize*, is really a very diverting farce. I obferved that, in England alfo, they reprefent fchoolmafters in ridiculous characters on the ftage; which though I am forry for, I own I do not wonder at, as the pedantry of fchool-mafters in England, they tell me, is carried, at leaft, as far, as it is elfewhere. The fame perfon who, in the play, performed the *fchool-fellow* of the *Nabob* with a great deal of nature, and original humour, here acted the part of the fchoolmafter, his name is *Edwin*, and he is, without doubt, one of the beft actors of all that I have feen.

This fchool-mafter is in love with a certain country girl, whofe name is *Cowflip*, to whom he makes a declaration of his paffion in a ftrange mythological, grammatical ftile and

E 2 manner,

manner, and to whom, among other fooleries, he sings, quite enraptured, the following air, and seems to work himself at least up to such a transport of passion, as quite over-powers him —He begins, you will observe, with the conjugation, and ends with the declensions and the genders, the whole is inimitably droll.

    " Amo, amas,
    " I love a lass,
    " She is so sweet and tender,
    " It is sweet *Cowslip's* Grace
    " In the Nominative Case,
    " And in the feminine Gender "

Those two sentences in particular, *in the Nominative Case*, and in the *Feminine Gender*, he affects to sing in a particularly languishing air, as if confident that it was irresistible. This Edwin, in all his comic characters, still preserves something so inexpressibly good tempered in his countenance, that notwithstanding all his burlesques, and even grotesque buffoonery, you cannot but be pleased with him. I own, I felt myself doubly interested for every character which he represented. Nothing could equal the tone and countenance of self-satisfaction, with which he answered one who asked him whether he was a

scholar ?

scholar? "Why, I was a master of scholars"
A Mrs Webb represented a cheesemonger,
and played the part of a woman of the lower
class, so naturally, as I have no where else
ever seen equalled.   Her huge, fat, and
lusty carcase, and the whole of her external
appearance seemed quite to be cut out for it.

Poor *Edwin* was obliged, as school-master,
to sing himself almost hoarse, as he sometimes
was called on to repeat his declension and
conjugation-songs, two or three times, only
because it pleased the upper gallery, or *the
gods*, as the English call them, to roar out,
encore! Add to all this he was farther forced
to thank them with a low bow for the great
honour done him by their applause

One of the highest comic touches in the
piece seemed to me to consist in a lye, which
always became more and more enormous in
the mouths of those who told it again, during
the whole of the piece   This kept the audi-
ence in almost a continual fit of laughter.
This farce is not yet printed, or I really think
I should be tempted to venture to make a
translation, or rather an imitation of it

The English Merchant, or, *The Scotchwoman*,
I have seen much better performed abroad,

E 3   than

than it was here   Mr. Fleck, at Hamburg, in particular, played the part of *The English Merchant* with more interest, truth and propriety, than one *Aickin* did here.   He seemed to me to fail totally in expressing the peculiar and original character of *Freeport*, instead of which, by his measured step, and deliberate, affected manner of speaking, he converted him into a mere fine gentleman.

The trusty old servant, who wishes to give up his life for his master, he too had the stately walk, or strut, of a minister.   The character of the *Newspaper Writer*, was performed by the same Mr. Palmer, who acted the part of the *Nabob*, but every one said, what I thought, that he made him far too much of a gentleman.   His person and his dress also were too handsome for the character.

The character of *Amelia* was performed by an actress, who made her first appearance on the stage, and from a timidity, natural on such an occasion, and not unbecoming, spoke rather low, so that she could not every where be heard, " *Speak louder! speak louder!* " cried out some rude fellow from the upper gallery, and she immediately, with infinite conde-
            scension,

scension, did all she could, and not unsuc-
cessfully, to please even an upper gallery
critic

The persons near me, in the pit, were
often extravagantly lavish of their applause.
They sometimes clapped a single solitary sen-
timent, that was almost as unmeaning as it
was short, if it happened to be pronounced
only with some little emphasis, or to contain
some little point, some popular doctrine, a
singularly pathetic stroke, or turn of wit.

The *Agreeable Surprise* was repeated, and I
saw it a second time with unabated pleasure.
It is become a favourite piece, and always
announced with the addition of *the favourite
musical farce*. The theatre appeared to me
somewhat larger than the one at Hamburg;
and the house was both times very full. Thus
much for English plays, play-houses, and
players.

English Customs and Education.

A few words more respecting pedantry.
I have seen the regulation of one seminary
of learning, here called *an Academy*. Of
these places of education, there is a prodigious number in London, though, notwith-

standing

ftanding their pompous names, they are in reality nothing more than fmall fchools fet up by private perfons, for children and young people.

One of the Englifhmen, who were my travelling companions, made me acquainted with a *Dr. G******, who lives near *P*————, and keeps an academy for the education of twelve young people, which number is here, as well as at our *Mr. Kumpe's*, never exceeded, and the fame plan has been adopted and followed by many others, both here, and elfewhere.

At the entrance I perceived over the door of the houfe a large board, and written on it, *Dr. G******'s *Academy*. Dr. G. received me with great courtefy as a foreigner, and fhewed me his fchool-room, which was furnifhed juft in the fame manner, as the claffes in our public fchools are, with benches and a profeffor's chair, or pulpit.

The ufher, at *Dr. G******'s, is a young clergyman, who, feated alfo in a chair, or defk, inftructs the boys in the Greek and Latin Grammars.

Such an under-teacher is called an ufher, and by what I can learn, is commonly a tor-
mented

mented being, exactly anfwering the exquifite defcription given of him in the Vicar of
Wakefield. We went in, during the hours
of attendance, and he was juft hearing the
boys decline their Latin, which he did in the
old jog-trot way, and I own it had an odd
found to my ears, when inftead of pronouncing, for example *viri veeres*, I heard them
fay *viri, of the man*, exactly according to the
Englifh pronunciation, and *viro, to the man*.
The cafe was juft the fame afterwards with the
Greek.

*Mr. G****:* invited us to dinner, when I
became acquainted with his wife, a very
genteel young woman, whofe behaviour to
the children was fuch, that fhe might be faid
to contribute more to their education than
any one elfe. The children drank nothing
but water For every boarder, Dr. G.
receives yearly no more than thirty pounds
fterling, which, however, he complained of,
as being two little —From forty to fifty
pounds is the moft that is generally paid in
thefe academies.

I told him of our improvements in the
manner of education, and alfo fpoke to him
of the apparent great worth of character of his

E 5   ufher.

ufher. He liftened very attentively, but feemed to have thought little himfelf on this fubject. Befoie and after dinner the Lord's Prayer was repeated in Fiench, which is done in feveral places, as if they weie eager not to wafte, without fome improvement, even this opportunity alfo, to piactife the French, and thus at once accomplifh two points. I aftei-wards told him my opinion of this fpecies of piayer, which, however, he did not take amifs.

After dinner the boys had leave to play in a very fmall yard, which in moft fchools, or academies, in the City of London, is the *ne plus ultra* of their play-ground in their hours of iecreation. But Mr. G^{****} has another gaiden at the end of the town, wheie he fometimes takes them to walk.

After dinner Mr. G^{****} himfelf inftructed the children in wiiting, arithmetic, and French, all which feemed to be well taught heie, efpecially wriring, in which the young people in England, far furpafs, I believe, all others. This may, peihaps, be ow-ing to their having occafion to learn only one fort of letters. As the Midfummer holi-days weie now appioaching (at which time

the

the children, in all the academies, go home for four weeks) every one was obliged with the utmoft care to copy a written model, in order to fhew it to their parents, becaufe this article is moft particularly examined, as every body can tell what is, or is not good writing. The boys knew all the rules of fyntax by heart.

All thefe academies are in general called boarding-fchools. Some few retain the old name of fchools only, though it is poffible, that, in real merit, they may excel the fo much-boafted of academies.

It is in general the clergy, who have fmall incomes, who fet up thefe fchools both in town and country, and grown up people, who are foreigners, are alfo admitted here to learn the Englifh language. Mr. G * * * * charged for board, lodging, and inftruction in the Englifh, two guineas a week. He, however, who is defirous of perfecting himfelf in the Englifh, will do better to go fome diftance into the country, and board himfelf with any clergyman, who takes fcholars, where he will hear nothing but Englifh fpoken, and may at every opportunity be taught both by young and old.

Their

There are in England, besides the two Univerfities, but few great fchools or colleges —In London there are only St. Paul's and Weftminfter fchools, the reft are almoft all private inftitutions, in which there reigns a kind of family education, which is certainly the moft natural, if properly conducted. Some few grammar fchools, or latin fchools, are notwithftanding here and there to be met with, where the mafter receives a fixed falary, befides the ordinary profits of the fchool, paid by the fcholars.

You fee in the ftreets, of London, great and little boys running about in long blue coats, which, like robes, reach quite down to the feet, and little white bands, fuch as the clergy wear. Thefe belong to a charitable inftitution, or fchool, which bears the name *of the Blue Coat School*. The finging of the chorifters in the ftreets, fo ufual with us, is not at all cuftomary here. Indeed, there is in England, or at leaft in London, fuch a conftant walking, riding, and driving up and down, in the ftreets, that it would not be very practicable. Parents, here in general, nay even thofe of the loweft claffes, feem to be kind and indulgent to their children, and do not, like our

common

common people, break their spirits too much by blows and sharp language. Children should certainly be enured early to set a proper value on themselves: whereas, with us, parents of the lower class bring up their children to the same slavery under which they themselves groan.

Notwithstanding the constant new appetites and calls of fashion, they here remain faithful to nature till a certain age —What a contrast, when I figure to myself our petted pale-faced Berlin boys, at six years old, with a large bag, and all the parade of grown up persons, nay, even with laced coats, and here, on the contrary, see nothing but fine, ruddy, slim, active boys, with their bosoms open, and their hair cut on their forehead, whilst behind it flows naturally in ringlets. It is something uncommon here to meet a young man, and more especially a boy, with a pale or sallow face, with deformed features, or disproportioned limbs.—With us, alas! it is not to be concealed, the case is very much otherwise: if it were not, handsome people would hardly strike us so very much as they do in this country.

This

This free, loofe, and natural drefs, is worn till they are eighteen, or even till they are twenty. It is then, indeed, difcontinued by the higher ranks, but with the common people it always remains the fame. They then begin to have their hair drefled, and curled with irons, to give the head a large bufhy appearance, and half their backs are covered with powder. I am obliged to remain ftill longer under the hands of an Englifh, than I was under a German, hair-drefler, and to fweat under his hot irons with which he curls my hair all over, in order that I may appear, among Englifhmen, fomewhat Englifh. I muft here obferve that the Englifh hair-drefles are alfo barbers, an office, however, which they perform very badly indeed; though I cannot but confider fhaving, as a far more proper employment for thefe petit maîtres, than it is for furgeons, who, you know, in our country are obliged to fhave us. It is incredible how much the Englifh at prefent frenchify themfelves, the only things yet wanting are bags and fwords, with which, at leaft, I have feen no one walking publicly, but I am told they are worn at Court.

In

In the morning, it is ufual to walk out in a fort of negligèe, or morning-drefs, your hair not dreffed, but merely rolled up in rollers, and in a frock and boots. In Weftminfter, the morning lafts till four, or five o'clock, at which time they dine, and fupper and going to bed are regulated accordingly. They generally do not breakfaft till ten o'clock. The farther you go from the Court, into the City, the more regular and domeftic the people become, and there they generally dine about three o'clock, *i. e.* as foon as the bufinefs or 'Change is over.

Trimmed fuits are not yet worn, and the moft ufual drefs is, in fummer, a fhort white waiftcoat, black breeches, white filk ftockings, and a frock, generally of very dark blue cloth, which looks like black, and the Englifh fcem, in general, to prefer dark colours. If you wifh to be full dreft you wear black. Officers rarely wear their uniforms, but drefs like other people, and are to be known to be officers only by a cockade in their hats.

It is a common obfervation, that the more folicitous any people are about drefs, the more effeminate they are. I attribute it entirely

to this idle adventitious paffion for finery,
that thefe people are become fo over and
above careful of their perfons; they are for
ever, and on every occafion, putting one
another on their guard, againft catching
cold, " you'll certainly catch cold," they
always tell you, if you happen to be a
little expofed to the draught of the air, or if
you be not clad, as they think, fufficiently
warm   The general topic of converfation
in fummer, is, on the important objects of
whether fuch and fuch an acquaintance be in
town, or fuch an one in the country.   Far
from blaming it, I think it natural and com-
mendable, that nearly one half of the inhabitants of this great city migrate into the
country in fummer. And into the country, I too,
though not a Londoner, hope foon to wander.

Electricity happens at prefent to be the
puppet-fhow of the Englifh   Whoever at
all underflands electricity, is fure of being
noticed and fuccefsful.—This, a certain Mr.
Katterfelto experiences, who gives himfelf
out for a *Pruffian,* fpeaks bad Englifh, and
underftands, befide the ufual electrical and
philofophical experiments, fome *leger-de-mom
tricks,* with which, (at leaft, according to the
papers)

papers) he fets the whole world in wonder. For, in almoft every newfpaper that appears, there are fome verfes on the great Katterfelto, which fome one or other of his hearers are faid to have made extempore Every fenfible perfon confiders Katterfelto, as a puppy, an ignoramus, a braggadocio, and an impoftor, notwithftanding which he has a number of followers. He has demonftrated to the people that the influenza, is occafioned by a fmall kind of infect, which poifons the air, and a noftrum, which he pretends to have found out, to prevent or deftroy it, is eagerly bought of him. A few days ago he put into the papers: " It is true, that Mr. Katterfelto " has always wifhed for cold and rainy wea- " ther, in order to deftroy the pernicious " infects in the air, but now, on the contrary, " he wifhes for nothing more than for fair " weather, as his Majefty and the whole royal " family have determined, the firft fine day, " to be eye witneffes of the great *wonder*, " which this learned philofopher will render " vifible to them." Yet all this while the royal family have not fo much as even *thought* of feeing the wonders of Mr. Katterfelto. This kind of rodomontade is very finely ex-

preffed

preffed in Englifh by the word *puff,* which in
its literal fenfe, fignifies a blowing, or violent guft of wind, and in the metaphorical
fenfe, a boafting, or bragging.

Of fuch *puffs* the Englifh newfpapers are
daily full; particularly of quack medicines,
and empirics, by means of which many a one
here (and among others, a German, who goes
by the name of the German Doctor) are become rich. An advertifement of a lottery in
the papers begins with capitals in this
manner:——" Ten Thoufand Pounds for a
" Sixpence! Yes, however aftonifhing it may
" feem, it is neverthelefs undoubtedly true
" that, for the fmall ftake of fixpence, ten
" thoufand pounds and other capital prizes
" may be won, &c."——But enough for this
time of the *puffs* of the Englifh.

I yefterday dined with the Rev. Mr.
Schrader, fon-in-law to profeffor Fofter of
Halle. He is chaplain to the German
chapel at St. James's, but befides himfelf, he
has a colleague, and a reader, who is alfo in
orders, but has only fifty pounds yearly falary. Mr. Schrader alfo inftructs the younger
princes and princeffes of the royal family in
their religion. At his houfe I faw the two

chaplains,

chaplains, Mr. Lindeman and Mr Kritter, who went with the Hanoverian troops to Minorca, and who were returned with the garrison. They were expofed to every danger along with the troops. The German clergy, as well as every other perfon in any public ftation, immediately under government, are obliged to pay a confiderable tax out of their falaries.

The Englifh clergy (and I fear, thofe ftill more particularly who live in London) are noticeable, and lamentably confpicuous, by a very free, fecular, and irregular way of life. Since my refidence in England, one has fought a duel in Hyde-Park, and fhot his antagonift. He was tried for the offence, and it was evident the judge thought him guilty of murder. but the jury declared him guilty only of manflaughter, and on this verdict, he was burnt in the hand, if that may be called burning which is done with a cold iron. This being a privilege which the nobility and clergy enjoy above other murderers.

Yefterday week, after I had preached for Mr. Wendeborne, we paffed an Englifh Church, in which, we underftood, the fermon

was

was not yet quite finished.   On this we went
in, and then I heard a young man preaching, with a tolerable good voice, and a
proper delivery, but, like the English in
general, his manner was unimpaffioned, and
his tone monotonous.   From the church we
went to a coffee-houfe, oppofite to it, and
there we dined.   We had not been long there
before the fame clergyman, whom we had juft
heard preaching, alfo came in   He called for
pen and ink, and haftily wrote down a few
pages on a long fheet of paper which he put
into his pocket ; I fuppofe it was fome rough
fketch, or memorandum, that occured to him
at that moment, and which he thus referved
for fome future fermon. He too ordered fome
dinner , which he had no fooner eat than he
returned immediately to the fame church. We
followed him, and he again mounted the
pulpit, where he drew from his pocket a
written paper, or book of notes, and delivered,
in all probability, thofe very words, which he
had juft before compofed in our prefence, at
the coffee-houfe.

In thefe coffee-houfes, however, there generally prevails a very decorous ftillnefs and
filence.   Every one fpeaks foftly to thofe only
who

who fit next him. The greater part read the newfpapers, and no one ever difturbs another. The room is commonly on the ground floor, and you enter it immediately from the ftreet, the feats are divided by wooden wainfcot partitions. Many letters and projects are here written and planned, and many of thofe that you find in the papers are dated from fome of thefe coffee-houfes. There is, therefore, nothing incredible, nor very extraordinary, in a perfon's compofing a fermon here, excepting that one would imagine it might have been done better at home, and certainly fhould not have thus been put off to the laft minute.

Another long walk that I have taken pretty often is through Hanover-fquare and Cavendifh-fquare, to Bullftrode-ftreet, near Paddington, where the Danifh Ambaffador lives, and where I have often vifited the Danifh Chargée d'Affaires, Mr. Schonborn. He is well known in Germany, as having attempted to tranflate Pindar into German. Befides this, and befides being known to be a man of genius, he is known to be a great proficient in moft of the branches of natural philofophy. I have fpent many very pleafant hours with him.

Sublime

Sublime poetry, and, in particular, odes, are his forte , there are indeed few departments of learning, in which he has not extenfive knowledge, and he is alfo well read in the Greek and Roman authors.   Every thing he fludies, he fludies merely from the love he bears to the fcience itfelf, and by no means for the love of fame.   One could hardly help faying it is a pity that fo excellent a man fhould be fo little known, were it not geneially the cafe with men of tranfcendent merit.   But what makes him ftill more valuable is his pure and open foul, and his amiable unaffected fimplicity of chaiacter, which has gained him the love and confidence of all who know him.   He has, heretofore, been Secretaiy to the Ambaffador at Algiers , and even heie, in London, when he is not occupied by the bufinefs arifing from his public ftation, he lives exceedingly retired, and devotes his time almoft entirely to the ftudy of the fciences. The moie agreeable I find fuch an acquaintance, the haider it will be for me to lofe, as I foon muft, his learned, his inftructive, and his friendly convei fation.

I have feen the large Fieemafon's Hall here, at the tavern of the fame name   This hall is of an aftonifhing height and bieadth,

and

and to me it looked almoſt like a church. The orcheſtra is very much raiſed, and from that you have a fine view of the whole hall, which makes a majeſtic appearance. The building is ſaid to have coſt an immenſe ſum. But to that the lodges in Germany alſo contributed. Free-maſonry ſeems to be held in but little eſtimation in England, perhaps, becauſe moſt of the lodges are now degenerated into mere drinking clubs; though, I hope, there ſtill are ſome, who aſſemble for nobler and more eſſential purpoſes. The Duke of Cumberland is now Grand Maſter.

LONDON, 20TH JUNE, 1782.

AT length, my determination of going into the country, takes effect; and I am to fet off this very afternoon in a ftage: fo that I now write to you my laft letter from London, I mean till I return from my pilgrimage, for as foon as ever I have got beyond the dangerous neighbourhood of London, I fhall certainly no longer fuffer myfelf to be cooped up in a poft-coach, but take my ftaff and purfue my journey on foot. In the mean time however I will relate to you, what I may either have forgotten to write before, or, what I have feen worth notice, within thefe few days laft paft, among which the foremoft is

St Paul's.

I muft own that, on my entrance into this maffy building, an uncommon vacancy, which feemed to reign in it, rather damped, than raifed, an impreffion of any thing majeftic in me. All around me I could fee nothing but immenfe bare walls and pillars. Above me, at an aftonifhing height, was the vaulted ftone roof, and beneath me, a plain, flat, even

4   floor,

floor, paved with marble. No altar was to be seen, or any other sign that this was a place where mankind assemble to adore the Almighty. For, the church itself, or properly that part of it where they perform divine service, seems as it were a piece stuck on or added to the main edifice, and is separated from the large round empty space by an iron gate, or door. Did the great architects, who adopted this stile of building, mean by this to say that such a temple is most proper for the adoration of the Almighty? If this was their aim, I can only say, I admire the great temple of nature, the azure vaulted sky, and the green carpet with which the earth is spread. This is truly a large temple, but then there is in it no void, no spot unappropriated, or unfilled but every where proofs in abundance of the presence of the Almighty. If however, mankind, in their honest ambition, to worship the great God of Nature, in a stile not wholly unsuitable to the great object of their reverence, and in their humble efforts at magnificence, aim, in some degree, to rival the magnificence of nature, particular pains should be taken to hit on something that might atone for the unavoid-

F

able

able lofs of the animation, and amplenefs, of
nature fomething in fhort, that fhould
clearly indicate the true and appropriated de-
fign and purpofe of fuch a building If, on
the other hand, I could be contented to confider St Paul's merely as a work of art, built
as if merely to fhew the amazing extent of human powers, I fhould certainly gaze at it
with admiration and aftonifhment. but then
I wifh rather to contemplate it with awe and
veneration. But, I perceive, I am wandering out of my way : St Paul's is here, as it is,
a noble pile, and not unworthy this great nation And even if I were fure that I could,
you would hardly thank me for fhewing you,
how it might have been ftill more worthy of
this intelligent people I make a confcience
however of telling you always, with fidelity,
what impreffion every thing I fee or hear,
makes on me at the time. For a fmall fum of
money, I was conducted all over the church,
by a man, whofe office it feemed to be, and he
repeated to me, I dare fay, exactly his leffon,
which no doubt he had perfectly got by rote;
of how many feet long and broad it was;
how many years it was in building, and in
what year built : much of this rigmarole
                              ftory,

ſtory, which, like a parrot, he repeated me-
chanically, I could willingly have diſpenſed
with. In the part that was ſeparated from the
reſt by the iron gate, above mentioned, was
what I call the church itſelf, furniſhed with
benches, pews, pulpit, and an altar, and on
each ſide, ſeats for the choriſters, as there
are in our cathedrals. This church ſeemed
to have been built purpoſely in ſuch a way,
that the Biſhop, or Dean, or Dignitary, who
ſhould preach there, might not be obliged to
ſtrain his voice too much. I was now conducted to that part, which is called the whiſ-
pering gallery, which is a circumference of
prodigious extent, juſt below the cupola.
Here I was directed to place myſelf in a part
of it directly oppoſite to my conductor, on
the other ſide of the gallery, ſo that we had
the whole breadth of the church between us,
and here as I ſtood, he, knowing his cue no
doubt, flung to the door, with all his force,
which gave a ſound that I could compare to
nothing leſs than a peal of thunder. I was
next deſired to apply my ear to the wall,
which, when I did, I heard the words of my
conductor · " *can you hear me?*" Which he
ſoftly whiſpered quite on the other ſide, as

F 2   plain

plain and as loud, as one commonly fpeaks to a deaf perfon. This fcheme to condenfe and invigorate found at fo great a diftance, is really wonderful. I once noticed fome found of the fame fort, in the fenatorial cellar at Bremen, but neither that, nor I believe any other in the world, can pretend to come in competition with this.

I now afcended feveral fteps to the great gallery, which runs on the outfide of the great dome, and here I remained nearly two hours, as I could hardly, in lefs time, fatisfy myfelf with the profpect of the various inte-refting objects that lay all round me, and which can no where be better feen, than from hence.

Every view, and every object I ftudied at-tentively, by viewing them again and again on every fide: for I was anxious to make a lafting impreffion of it on my imagination. Below me, lay fteeples, houfes, and palaces in countlefs numbers, the fquares with their grafs plots in their middle that lay agreeably difperfed and intermixed, with all the huge clufters of buildings, forming, mean-while, a pleafing contraft, and a relief to the jaded eye.

At

At one end rofe the Tower, itfelf a city, with a wood of mafts behind it, and at the other Weftminfter Abbey with its fteeples. There I beheld, clad in fmiles, thofe beautiful green hills, that fkirt the environs of Paddington and Iflington: here on the oppofite bank of the Thames, lay Southwark, the City itfelf it feems to be impoffible for any eye to take in entirely, for, with all my pains, I found it impoffible to afcertain, either where it ended, or where the circumjacent villages began: far as the eye could reach, it feemed to be all one continued chain of buildings.

I well remember how large I thought Berlin, when I firft faw it, from the fteeple of St. Mary, and from the Temple Yard Hills: but how did it now fink and fall in my imagination, when I compared it with London!

It is however idle and vain to attempt giving you, in words, any defcription, however faint and imperfect, of fuch a profpect as I have juft been viewing. He who wifhes at one view to fee a world in miniature, muft come to the dome of St Paul's.

The

The roof of St Paul's itfelf with its two leffer fteeples, lay below me, and as I fancied, looked fomething like the back ground of a fmall ridge of hills, which you look down upon, when you have attained the fummit of fome huge rock or mountain I fhould gladly have remained here fometime longer, but a guft of wind which, in this fituation, was fo powerful, that it was hardly poffible to withftand it, drove me down.

Notwithftanding that St. Paul's is itfelf very high, the elevation of the ground on which it ftands, contributes greatly to its elevation.

The church of St Peter at Berlin, notwith-ftanding the total difference between them in the ftile of building, appears, in fome ref-pects, to have a great refemblance to St. Paul's, in London   At leaft its large high black roof, rifes above the other furrounding buildings juft as St. Paul's does

What elfe I faw in this ftately cathedral, was only a wooden model of this very edifice, which was made before the church was built, and which fuggefts fome not unpleafing reflections, when one compares it with the enormous building itfelf

The church yard is enclofed with an iron rail,

rail, and it appears a confiderable diftance, if you go all round.

Owing to fome caufe or other, the fight of St. Paul's ftrikes you, as being confined, and it is certain, that this beautiful church is on every fide clofely furrounded by houfes.

A marble ftatue of Queen Anne, in an en-clofed piece of ground in the weft front of the church, is fomething of an ornament to that fide.

The fize of the bell of St. Paul's is alfo wor-thy of notice, as it is reckoned one of thofe that are deemed the largeft in Europe. It takes its place they fay next to that at Vienna.

Every thing that I faw in St Paul's coft me only a little more than a fhilling, which I paid in pence and halfpence, according to a regu-lated price, fixed for every different curiofity.

Weftminfter Abbey.

On a very gloomy difmal day, juft fuch an one as it ought to be, I went to fee Weft-minfter Abbey.

I entered at a fmall door, which brought me immediately to *the poets' corner,* where the monuments and bufts of the principal

F 4   poets,

poets, artists, generals, and great men, are placed.

Not far from the door, immediately on my entrance, I perceived the statue of Shakespeare, as large as life, with a band &c in the dress usual in his time.

A passage out of one of Shakespeare's own plays, (the tempest,) in which he describes in the most solemn and affecting manner, the end, or the dissolution, of all things, is here, with great propriety, put up as his epitaph; as though none but Shakespeare could do justice to Shakespeare.

Not far from this immortal bard is Rowe's monument, which, as is intimated in the few lines that are inscribed as his epitaph, he himself had desired to be placed there.

At no great distance, I saw the bust of that amiable writer, Goldsmith, to whom, as well as to Butler, whose monument is in a distant part of the Abbey, though they had scarcely necessary bread to eat during their life time, handsome monuments are now raised   Here, too you see, almost in a row, the monuments of Milton, Dryden, Gay, and Thompson. The inscription on Gay's tomb-stone is, if not

actually

actually immoral, yet futile and weak; though he is said to have written it himself,

" Life is a jest, and all things shew it,
" I thought so once, but now I know it "

Our Handel has also a monument here, where he is represented as large as life.

An actress, Pritchard, and Booth, an actor, have also very distinguished monuments erected here to their memories.

For Newton, as was proper, there is a very costly one. It is above, at the entrance of the choir, and exactly opposite to this, at the end of the church, another is erected, which refers you to the former.

As I passed along the side walls of West-minster Abbey, I hardly saw any thing but marble monuments of great admirals, but which were all too much loaded with finery and ornaments, to make, on me at least, the intended impression.

I always returned with most pleasure to *the poets' corner*, where the most sensible, the most able, and most learned men, of the different ages were re-assembled, and particularly where the elegant simplicity of the monuments,

F 5   made

made an elevated and affecting impreſſion on the mind, while a perfect recollection of ſome favourite paſſage, of a Shakeſpeare, or Milton, recurred to my idea, and ſeemed for a moment to re-animate and bring back the ſpirits of thoſe truly great men

Of Addiſon and Pope I have found no monuments here. The vaults where the Kings are buried, and ſome others things worth notice in the Abbey, I have not yet ſeen, but perhaps I may at my return to London from the country.

I have made every neceſſary preparation for this journey. In the firſt place, I have an accurate map of England in my pocket, beſides an excellent book of the roads, which Mr Pointer, the Engliſh Merchant to whom I am recommended, has lent me· The title is, " A New and accurate deſcription of all the " direct, and principal croſs Roads in Great- " Britain." This book, I hope, will be of great ſervice to me in my ramblings

I was for a long time undecided which way I ſhould go, whether to the Iſle of Wight, to Portſmouth, or to Derbyſhire, which is famous for its natural curioſities, and alſo for its ro-

romantic fituation. At length I have determined on Derbyfhire.

During my abfence I leave my trunk at
Mr Mulhaufen's, (one of Mr. Pointer's fe-
nior partners) that I may not be at the need-
lefs expence of paying for my lodging without
making ufe of it. This Mr Pointer lived
long in Germany, and is politely partial to
us and our language, and fpeaks it well. He
is a well bred, and fingularly obliging man,
and one who poffeffes a vaft fund of information, and a good tafte. I cannot but feel
myfelf happy in having obtained a recommendation to fo accomplifhed a man. I got
it from Meffrs Perfent and Dorner, to whom
I had the honour to be recommended by Mr.
von Taubenheim, Privy Counfellor at Berlin.
Thefe recommendations have been of infinite
ufe to me.

I propofe to go to day as far as Richmond,
for which place a Stage fets out about two
o'clock from fome inn, not far from the
New Church in the Strand. Four guineas,
fome linen, my Englifh book of the roads,
and a map and pocket-book, together with
Milton's Paradife Loft, which I muft put in my

F 6   pocket,

pocket, compofe the whole of my equipage; and I hope to walk very lightly with it. But it now ftrikes half paft one, and of courfe it it is time for me to be at the ftage. Fore-well! I will write to you again from Rich-mond.

RICHMOND, 21ST JUNE, 1782.

YESTERDAY afternoon I had the luxury, for the firft time, of being driven in an Englifh ftage. Thefe coaches are at leaft in the eyes of a foreigner, quite elegant, lined in the infide, and with two feats large enough to accommodate fix perfons: but it muft be owned, when the carriage is full, the company are rather crowded.

At the White-hart from whence the coach fets out, there was, at firft, only an elderly lady who got in, but as we drove along, it was foon filled, and moftly by ladies, there being only one more gentleman, and myfelf. The converfation of the ladies among themfelves, who appeared to be a little acquainted with each other, feemed to me to be but very infipid and tirefome. All I could do, was, I drew out my book of the roads, and marked the way we were going

Before you well know that you are out of London, you are already in Kenfington and Hammerfmith, becaufe there are, all the way, houfes on both fides, after you are out of the City, juft as you may remember the cafe is

with

with us when you drive from Berlin to Schonebeig, although in point of profpect, houfes, and ftreets, the diffeience, no doubt, is piodigious

It was a fine day, and theie were various delightful piofpects on both fides, on which the eye would willingly have dwelt longer, had not our coach rolled on paft them, fo provokingly quick. It appeared fomewhat fingular to me, when, at a few miles fiom London, I faw at a diftance a beautiful white houfe, and perceived on the high-road, on which w weie diiving, a direction-poft, on which weie wiitten thefe woids. " that gieat white houfe, at a diftance, is a boaiding fchool !"

The man, who was with us in the coach, pointed out to us the countiy feats of the loids and gieat people, by which we paffed, and enteitained us with all kind of ftoiies of rob-beries, which had been committed on travel-leis, hereabouts fo that the ladies at laft began to be iather afiaid on which he began to ftand up foi the fuperior honoui of the Englifh iobbers, when compared with the French the foinei he faid iobbed only, the lattei, both robbed and muideied.

Not-

Notwithſtanding this, there are in England another ſpecies of villains, who alſo murder, and that oftentimes for the mereſt trifle, of which they rob the perſon murdered. Theſe are called *Footpads*, and are the loweſt claſs of Engliſh rogues, amongſt whom in general there reigns ſomething like ſome regard to character.

The higheſt order of thieves are the pickpockets, or cutpurſes, whom you find every where, and ſometimes even in the beſt companies. They are generally well and handſomely dreſſed, ſo that you take them to be perſons of rank, as indeed may ſometimes be the caſe. perſons who, by extravagance and exceſſes, have reduced themſelves to want, and find themſelves obliged at laſt to have recourſe to pilfering and thieving.

Next to them, come the highwaymen, who rob on horſe-back, and often, they ſay, even with unloaded piſtols they terrify travellers, in order to put themſelves in poſſeſſion of their purſes. Among theſe perſons however there are inſtances of true greatneſs of ſoul, there are numberleſs inſtances of their returning a part of their booty, where the party robbed has appeared to be particularly

dif-

diſtreſſed, and they are ſeldom guilty of murder.

Then comes the third and loweſt, and worſt of all thieves and rogues, the foot pads before mentioned, who are on foot and often murder in the moſt inhuman manner, for the ſake of only a few ſhillings, any unfortunate people who happen to fall in their way. Of this ſeveral mournful inſtances may be read almoſt daily in the Engliſh papers. Probably they murder, becauſe they cannot, like highwaymen, aided by their horſes, make a rapid flight, and therefore ſuch peſts are frequently pretty eaſily purſued and taken, if the perſon robbed gives information of his robbery in time.

But, to return to our ſtage I muſt obſerve, that they have here a curious way of riding. not in, but upon, a ſtage-coach. Perſons, to whom it is not convenient to pay a full price, inſtead of the inſide, ſit on the top of the coach, without any ſeats or even a rail. By what means paſſengers thus faſten themſelves ſecurely on the roof of theſe vehicles, I know not, but you conſtantly ſee numbers ſeated there, apparently at their eaſe, and in perfect ſafety.

This

This they call riding on the outside, for which they pay only half as much as those pay, who are within· we had at present six of these passengers over our heads, who, when we alighted frequently made such a noise, and bustle, as sometimes almost frightened us.   He who can properly balance himself, rides not incommodiously on the outside: and in summer time, in fine weather, on account of the prospects, it certainly is more pleasant than it is within: excepting that the company is generally low, and the dust is likewise more troublesome than in the inside, where, at any rate, you may draw up the windows according to your pleasure.

In Kensington where we stopped, a Jew applied for a place along with us, but as there was no seat vacant in the inside, he would not ride on the outside, which seemed not quite to please my travelling companions. They could not help thinking it somewhat preposterous, that a Jew should be ashamed to ride on the outside, or on any side, and in any way, since, as they added, he was nothing more than a Jew.   This antipathy and prejudice against the Jews, I have noticed to be far more common here, than it is even

with

with us, who certainly are not partial to them

Of the beautiful country feats and villas which we now paſſed, I could only through the windows of our coach gain a partial and indiſtinct proſpect, which led me to wiſh, as I ſoon moſt earneſtly did, to be releaſed from this moveable priſon. Towards evening we arrived at Richmond. In London, before I ſet out, I had paid one ſhilling: another was now demanded, ſo that, upon the whole, from London, to Richmond, the paſſage in the ſtage coſts juſt two ſhillings.

As ſoon as I had alighted at an inn and had drank my tea, I went out immediately to ſee the town and the circumjacent country.

Even this town, though hardly out of ſight of London, is more countryfied, pleaſanter, and more cheerful than London, and the houſes do not ſeem to be ſo much blackened by ſmoke The people alſo appeared to me here more ſociable, and more hoſpitable. I ſaw ſeveral ſitting on benches before their doors, to enjoy the cool breeze of the evening On a large green area, in the middle of the town, a number of boys and even young men, were enjoying themſelves, and

playing

playing at trap-ball. In the streets there reigned here, compared to London, a pleasing rural tranquillity, and I breathed a purer and fresher air.

I now went out of the town over a bridge, which lies across the Thames, and where you pay a penny, as often as you pass over it The bridge is lofty, and built in the form of an arch, and from it you enter immediately into a most charming valley, that winds all along the banks of the Thames.

It was evening, the sun was just shedding her last parting rays on the valley · but such an evening, and such a valley ! O, it is impossible I should ever forget them. The terrace at Richmond does assuredly afford one of the finest prospects in the world. Whatever is charming in nature, or pleasing in art, is to be seen here. Nothing I had ever seen, or ever can see elsewhere, is to be compared to it My feelings, during the few short enraptured minutes that I stood there, it is impossible for any pen to describe.

One of my first sensations was, chagrin and sorrow for the days and hours I had wasted in London, and I vented a thousand bitter reproaches on my irresolution, that I had not

long

long ago quitted that huge dungeon, to come here, and pass my time in paradise.

Yes, my friend, whatever be your ideas of paradise, and how luxuriantly foever it may be depictured to your imagination, I venture to foretell, that here you will be fure to find all thofe ideas realized In every point of view, Richmond is affuredly one of the firft fituations in the world.   Here it was that Thomfon and Pope gleaned from nature all thofe beautiful paffages with which their inimitable writings abound !

Inftead of the inceffant, diftreffing noife in London, I faw here at a diftance, fundry little family parties, walking arm in arm along the banks of the Thames.   Every thing breathed a foft and pleafing calm, which warmed my heart, and filled it with fome of the moft pleafing fenfations, of which our nature is fufceptible.

Beneath, I trod on that frefh, even, and foft verdure which is to be feen only in England on one fide of me lay a wood, than which nature cannot produce a finer, and on the other, Thames with its fhelvy bank, and charming lawns, rifing like an amphitheatre, along which, here and there, one efpies a pic-

tu refque

turefque white houfe, afpiring, in majeftic fimplicity, to pierce the dark foliage of the furrounding trees, thus, ftudding, like ftars in
the galaxy, the rich expanfe of this charming
vale.

Sweet Richmond! never, no never fhall I
forget that lovely evening, when from thy
fairy hills thou didft fo hofpitably fmile on me,
a poor lonely, infignificant ftranger! As I
traverfed to and fro thy meads, thy little fwel-
ling hills, and flowery dells, and above all,
that queen of all rivers, thy own majeftic
Thames, I forgot all fublunary cares, and
thought only of heaven and heavenly things.
Happy, thrice happy am I, I again and again
exclaimed, that I am no longer in yon gloomy
city, but here in *Elyfium*, in Richmond!

O ye copfy hills, ye green meadows, and
ye rich ftreams in this bleffed country,—how
have ye enchanted me! Still however, let me
recollect, and refolve, as I firmly do, that
even ye fhall not prevent my return to thofe
barren and dufty lands, where my, perhaps a
lefs indulgent, deftiny has placed me, and
where, in the due difcharge of all the arduous
and important duties of that humble function,
to which providence has called me, I muft

and

and I will faithfully exert my beft talents, and
in that exertion find pleafure, and I truft,
happinefs. In every future moment of my
life, however, the recollection of this fcene,
and the feelings it infpired, fhall cheer my
labours, and invigorate my efforts.

These were fome of my reflections, my
deareft friend, during my folitary walk. Of
the evening I paffed at Richmond, I fpeak
feebly, when I content myfelf with faying only,
it was one of the pleafanteft I ever fpent in
my life.

I now refolved to go to bed early, with a
firm purpofe of alfo rifing early the next
day, to revifit this charming walk. For I
thought to myfelf, I have now feen this *Tempe*
of the modern world imperfectly, I have
feen it only by moon-light how much more
charming muft it be, when gliftening with
the morning dew ! Thefe fond hopes alas !
were all difappointed. In all great fchemes of
enjoyment, it is I believe, no bad way always
to figure to yourfelf fome poffible evil that
may arife, and to anticipate a difappointment.
If I had done fo, I fhould not perhaps have
felt the mortification I then experienced, quite
fo pungent. By fome means or other I ftaid

I   too

too long out, and so when I returned to Richmond, I had forgot the name and the sign of the inn, where I had before stopped, it cost me no little trouble to find it again.

When at last, I got back, I told the people, what a sweet walk I had had, and they then spoke much of a prospect from a neighbouring hill, known by the name of *Richmond Hill*, which was the very same hill, from the top of which I had just been gazing, at the houses in the vale the preceding evening. From this same hill, therefore, I resolved the next morning to see the sun rise.

The landlady of this house was a notable one, and talked so much and so loud to her servants, that I could not get to sleep, till it was pretty late. However, I was up next morning at three o'clock: and was now particularly sensible of the great inconveniences they sustain in England by their bad custom of rising so late. for, as I was the only one in this family who was up, I could not get out of the house. This obliged me to spend three most irksome and heavy hours till six o'clock, however, a servant, at length, opened the door, and I rushed out, to climb Richmond-hill. To my

my infinite difappointment, within the fpace
of an hour, the fky had become overcaft,
and it was now fo cloudy, that I could not
even fee, nor of courfe enjoy, one half of the
delightful profpect that lay before me.

On the top of this hill is an alley of chefnut-
trees, under which here and there feats are
placed. Behind the alley is a row of well
built gentlemen's country feats one does not
wonder to fee it thus occupied, befides the
pure air, the profpect exceeds every thing elfe
of the kind in the world. I never faw a palace, which (if I were the owner of it) I
would not give for any of the houfes I now
faw on Richmond Terrace.

The defcent of the hill to the Thames is
covered with verdure The Thames, at the
foot of it, forms near a femi-circle, in which
it feems to embrace woody plains, with meadows and country feats in its bofom On
one fide you fee the town with its magnificent
bridge, and on the other a dark wood.

At a diftance you could perceive peeping
out among the meadows and woods fundry
fmall villages, fo that notwithftanding the
dulnefs of the weather, this profpect, even
now, was one of the fineft I had ever feen.

2   But

But what is the reason, that yesterday evening my feelings were far more acute and lively, the impressions made on me much stronger, when from the vale I viewed the hill, and fancied that there was in it every thing that was delightful, than they are this morning, when from the hill itself I overlooked the vale, and knew pretty exactly what it contained?

I have now finished my breakfast; and, once more seize my staff, (the only companion I have) and now again, set out on this romantic journey on foot. From Windsor you shall hear more of me.

G   *WINDSOR,*

WINDSOR, 13TH JUNE.

I HAVE already, my deareſt friend, now
that I write to you from hence, experienced
ſo many inconveniences as a traveller on foot,
that I am at ſome loſs to determine, whether
or no, I ſhall go on with my journey in the
ſame manner.

A traveller on foot in this country ſeems to
be confidered as a fort of wild man, or an
out-of-the-way-being, who is ſtared at, pitied,
ſufpected, and ſhunned by every body that
meets him. At leaſt this has hitherto been
my cafe, on the road from Richmond to
Windfor.

My hoſt at Richmond, yeſterday morning,
could not ſufficiently expreſs his furprize, that
I intended to venture to walk as far as Oxford, and ſtill farther. He however was ſo
kind as to fend his fon, a clever little boy, to
ſhew me the road leading to Windfor.

At firſt I walked along a very pleaſant footway by the ſide of the Thames, where cloſe
to my right lay the king's garden. On the
oppoſite bank of the Thames was *Iſleworth*,
a ſpot that ſeemed to be diſtinguiſhed by

ſome

some elegant gentlemen's country-seats and gardens. Here I was obliged to ferry the river, in order to get into the Oxford road, which also leads to Windsor.

When I was on the other side of the water, I came to a house, and asked a man who was standing at the door, if I was on the right road to Oxford. " Yes," said he, " but you want a " carriage to carry you thither ·" when I answered him, that I intended walking it, he looked at me significantly, shook his head, and went into the house again

I was now on the road to Oxford. It is a charming fine broad road, and I met on it carriages without number; which, however, on account of the heat, occasioned a dust that was extremely troublesome and disagreeable. The fine green hedges, which border the roads in England, contribute greatly to render them pleasant. This was the case in the road I now travelled: for, when I was tired, I sad down in the shade under one of these hedges, and read Milton. But this relief was soon rendered disagreeable to me, for, those who rode, or drove, past me, stared at me with astonishment, and made many significant gestures, as if they thought my head

G 2   deranged.

deranged. So fingular muft it needs have appeared to them to fee a man fitting along the fide of a public road, and reading. I therefore found myfelf obliged when I wifhed to reft myfelf and read, to look out for a retired fpot in fome by-lane or crofs-road.

When I again walked, many of the coachmen who drove by, called out to me, ever and anon, and afked if I would not ride on the outfide; and when, every now and then, a farmer on horfeback met me, he faid, and feemingly with an air of pity for me,—" 'tis warm walking, fir!" and when I paffed through a village, every old woman teftified her pity by an exclamation of—*Good God!*

As far as Hounflow, the way was very pleafant. afterwards I thought it not quite fo good. It lay acrofs a common, which was of a confiderable extent, and bare, and naked; excepting that, here and there, I faw fheep feeding.

I now began to be rather tired; when, to my aftonifhment, I faw a tree in the middle of the common, that ftood quite folitary, and fpread a fhade like an arbour around it: at the bottom, round the trunk, a bench was placed, on which one may fit down, beneath

the

the shade of this tree, I reposed myself a little, read some of Milton, and made a note in my memorandum-book, that I would remember this tree, which had so charitably and hospitably received under it's shade, a weary traveller.   This, you see, I have now done.

The short English miles are delightful for walking, you are always pleased to find, every now and then, in how short a time you have walked a mile. though, no doubt, a mile is every where a mile.   I walk but a moderate pace, and can accomplish four English miles in an hour, it used to take me pretty nearly the same time for one German mile   Now it is a pleasing exchange to find, that in two hours I can walk eight miles.   And now I fancy, I was about seventeen miles from London, when I came to an inn, where, for a little wine and water I was obliged to pay sixpence.   An Englishman, who happened to be sitting by the side of the innkeeper, found out that I was a German, and of course from the country of his queen: in praise of whom he was quite lavish; observing more than once, that England never had had such a queen, and would not easily get such another.

It

It now began to grow hot.   On the left
hand, almoft clofe to the high-road, I met
with a fingularly clear rivulet.   In this I
bathed, and was much refrefhed, and afterwards with frefh alacrity, continued my
journey.

I had now got over the common: and
was, once more, in a country rich and well
cultivated, beyond all conception. This continued to be the cafe as far as *Slough*, which is
twenty miles and a half from London, on the
way to Oxford; and from which to the left
there is a road leading to Windfor, whofe
high white caftle I have already feen at a
diftance.

I made no ftay here, but went directly to
the right, along a very pleafant high-road,
between meadows and green hedges, towards
Windfor, where I arrived about noon.

It ftrikes a foreigner as fomething particular and unufual, when, on paffing through
thefe fine Englifh towns, he obferves none of
thofe circumftances, by which the towns in
Germany are diftinguifhed from the villages,
no walls, no gates, no fentries, nor garrifons.
No ftern examiner comes here to fearch and
infpect us, or our baggage, no imperious

guard

guard here demands a fight of our paffports: perfectly free and unmolefted, we here walk through villages and towns, as unconcerned, as we fhould through an houfe of our own.

Juft before I got to Windfor, I paffed Eton-College, one of the firft public fchools in England, and perhaps in the world. I have before obferved, that there are in England fewer of thefe great fchools than one might expect. It lay on my left, and on the right, directly oppofite to it, was an inn, into which I went

I fuppofe it was during the hour of recreation, or in play time, when I got to Eton · for I faw the boys, in the yard before the college, which was enclofed by a low wall, in great numbers, walking and running up and down.

Their drefs ftruck me particularly: from the biggeft to the leaft, they all wore black cloaks, or gowns, over coloured cloaths; through which there was an aperture for their arms They alfo wore, befides, a fquare hat, or cap, that feemed to be covered with velvet, fuch as our clergymen in many places wear.

They were differently employed: fome talking together, fome playing; and fome had

G 4

had their books in their hands, and were reading, but, I was foon obliged to get out of their
fight, they ftaied at me fo, as I came along,
all over duft, with my ftick in my hand.

As I enteied the inn and defiied to have
fomething to eat, the countenance of the
waiter foon gave me to underftand, that I
fhould theie find no very friendly reception.
Whatever I got, they feemed to give me,
with fuch an air, as fhewed too plainly how
little they thought of me, and as if they
confideied me but as a beggai. I muft do
them the juftice to own, however, that they
fuffered me to pay like a gentleman. No
doubt this was the firft time, this pert be-
powdered puppy had ever been called on to
wait on a poor devil, who enteied their place
on foot I was tired, and afked for a bed-
room, where I might fleep. They fhewed
me into one, that much iefembled a piifon
for malefactois. I iequefted that I might have
a better room at night. On which, without
any apology, they told me, that they had no
intention of lodging me, as they had no ioom
for fuch guefts, but that I might go back to
Slough, where veiy probably I might get a
night's lodging.

With

With money in my pocket, and a confci-
oufnefs moreover that I was doing nothing
that was either imprudent, unworthy, or really
mean, I own it mortified and vexed me, to
find myfelf obliged to put up with this impudent ill ufage from people, who ought to reflect, that they are but the fervants of the
public, and little likely to recommend themfelves to the high, by being infolent to the
low. They made me, however, pay them
two fhillings for my dinner and coffee; which
I had juft thrown down, and was preparing to
fhake off the duft from my fhoes, and quit
this inhofpitable St. Chriftopher, when the
green hills of Windfor fmiled fo friendly
upon me, that they feemed to invite me firft
to vifit them.

And now, trudging through the ftreets of
Windfor, I at length mounted a fort of hill:
a fteep path led me on to its fummit, clofe to
the walls of the caftle, where I had an uncommonly extenfive, and fine profpect, which fo
much raifed my heart, that, in a moment, I
forgot not only the infults of waiters and
tavern-keepers, but the hardfhip of my lot,
in being obliged to travel in a manner that
expofed me to the fcorn of a people whom

G 5   I wifhed.

I wifhed to refpect. Below me lay the moft beautiful landfcapes in the world , all the rich fcenery that nature, in her beft attire, can exhibit. Here were the fpots, that furnifhed thofe delightful themes, of which the mufe of Denham and Pope made choice. I feemed to view a whole world at once, rich and beautiful, beyond conception. At that moment, what more could I have wifhed for !

And the venerable caftle, that royal edifice, which, in every part of it, has ftrong traces of antiquity, fmiles through its green trees, like the ferene countenance of fome hoary fage, who, by the vigour of an happy conftitution, ftill retains many of the charms of youth.

Nothing infpired me with more veneration and awe, than the fine old building, St. George's church , which, as you come down from the caftle, is on your right. At the fight of it, paft centuries feemed to revive in my imagination.

But I will fee no more of thofe fights which are fhewn you by one of thofe venal praters, who ten times a day, parrot-wife, repeat over the fame dull leffon they have got by heart. The furly fellow, who, for a fhilling, conducted me round the church, had nearly, with

his

his chattering, deftroyed the fineft impreffions. Henry the Eighth, Charles the Firft, and Edward the Fourth, are buried here. After all, this church, both within and without, has a moft melancholy and difmal appearance.

They were building at, what is called, the queen's palace, and prodigious quantities of materials are provided for that purpofe.

I now went down a gentle declivity into the delightful park at Windfor. at the foot of which, it looks fo fombrous and gloomy, that I could hardly help fancying, it was fome vaft old gothic temple. This foreft certainly, in point of beauty, furpaffes every thing of the kind you can figure to yourfelf. To its own charms, when I faw it, there were added a moft pleafing and philofophical folitude; the coolnefs of an evening breeze; all aided by the foft founds of mufic, which, at this diftance from the caftle, from whence it iffued, was inexpreffibly fweet. It threw me into a fort of enthufiaftic and pleafing reverie, which made me ample amends for the fatigues, difcourtefies, and continued crofs accidents, I had encountered in the courfe of the day.

I now

I now left the foreſt; the clock ſtruck ſix,, and the workmen were going home from their work.

I have forgot to mention the large round tower of the caſtle; which is alſo a very ancient building. The roads that lead to it,, are, all along their ſides planted with ſhrubs; theſe being modern and lively, make a pleaſing, contraſt to the fine old moſſy walls. On the top of this tower the flag of Great-Britain is uſually diſplayed, which however, as it was now late in the evening, was taken in.

As I came down from the caſtle, I ſaw the king driving up to it, in a very plain, two-wheeled, open carriage. The people here were politer, than I uſed to think they were in London: for, I did not ſee a ſingle perſon, high or low, who did not pull off their hats, as their ſovereign paſſed them.

I was now again in Windſor; and found myſelf not far from the caſtle, oppoſite to a very capital inn, where I ſaw many officers and ſeveral perſons of conſequence going in and out. And here, at this inn, contrary to all expectation, I was received by the land-lord, with great civility, and even kindneſs; very contrary to the haughty and inſolent airs,

                                    which

which the upstart at the other, and his jack-anapes of a waiter, there thought fit to give themselves.

However, it seemed to be my fate to be still a scandal, and an eye-sore to all the waiters. The maid, by the order of her master, shewed me a room where I might adjust my dress a little, but I could hear her mutter and grumble, as she went along with me. Having put myself a little to rights, I went down into the coffee-room, which is immediately at the entrance of the house, and told the landlord, that I thought I wished to have yet one more walk. On this, he obligingly directed me to stroll down a pleasant field behind his house, at the foot of which, he said, I should find the Thames, and a good bathing place.

I followed his advice, and this evening was, if possible, finer than the preceding. Here again, as I had been told I should, I found the Thames, with all its gentle windings, Windsor, shone nearly as bright over the green vale, as those charming houses on Richmond-Hill, and the verdure was not less soft and delicate. The field I was in, seemed to slope a little towards the Thames. I seated myself myfelf near a bufh, and there waited the going down of the fun. At a diftance I faw a number of people bathing in the Thames. When, after fun-fet, they were a little dif-perfed, I drew near the fpot I had been di-rected to · and here, for the firft time, I fported in the cool tide of the Thames. The bank was fteep, but my landlord had dug fome fleps that went down into the water, which is extremely convenient for thofe who cannot fwim. Whilft I was there, a couple of fmart lively apprentice boys came alfo, from the town, who, with the greateft expedition, threw off their cloaths and leathern aprons, and plunged themfelves, head foremoft, into the water, where they oppofed the tide with their finewy arms, till they were tired. They ad-vifed me with much natural civility, to untie my hair, and that then, like them, I might plunge into the ftream, head foremoft.

Refrefhed and ftrengthened by this cool bath, I took a long walk by moon-light on the banks of the Thames, to my left were the towers of Windfor, before me a little village, with a fteeple, the top of which peeped out among the green trees ; at a diftance two inviting hills, which I was to

clumb

climb in the morning, and around me the green corn-fields, Oh! how indescribably beautiful was this evening, and this walk! at a distance among the houses, I could easily descry the inn where I lodged, and where I seemed to myself at length to have found a place of refuge, and an home: and I thought, if I could but stay there, I should not be very sorry, if I were never to find another.

How soon did all these pleasing dreams vanish! On my return, the waiters (who from my appearance, too probably expected but a trifling reward for their attentions to me) received me gruffly, and as if they were sorry to see me again. This was not all: I had the additional mortification to be again roughly accosted by the cross maid, who had before shewn me to the bed-chamber; and who, dropping a kind of half courtesy, with a suppressed laugh, sneeringly told me, I might look out for another lodging, as I could not sleep there, since the room she had by mistake shewn me, was already engaged. It can hardly be necessary to tell you, that I loudly protested against this sudden change. At length the landlord came and I appealed to him: and he with great courtesy, immediately

diately defired another room to be fhewn me; in which, however, there were two beds, fo that I was obliged to admit a companion. Thus was I very near being a fecond time turned out of an inn.

Directly under my room, was the tap-room · from which I could plainly hear too much of the converfation of fome low people, who were drinking and finging fongs, in which, as far as I could underftand them, there were many paffages at leaft as vulgar and nonfenfical as ours.

This company, I gueffed, confifted chiefly of foldiers, and low fellows. I was hardly well lulled to fleep by this hurley-burley, when my chum (probably one of the drinking party below) came ftumbling into the room and againft my bed. At length, though not without fome difficulty, he found his own bed; into which he threw himfelf juft as he was, without ftaying to pull off either cloaths or boots.

This morning I rofe very early, as I had propofed, in order to climb the two hills, which yefterday prefented me with fo inviting a profpect, and in particular that one of them, on the fummit of which an high white houfe

appeared.

appeared among the dark green trees, the other was close by.

I found no regular path leading to these hills; and therefore went straight forward, without minding roads; only keeping in view the object of my aim. This certainly created me some trouble. I had sometimes an hedge, and sometimes a bog to walk round, but at length I had attained the foot of the so earnestly wished for hill, with the high white house on its summit, when, just as I was going to ascend it, and was already pleasing myself in the idea with the prospect from the white house, behold I read these words on a board: *Take care! there are steel traps and spring guns here.* All my labour was lost, and I now went round to the other hill, but here were also *steel traps* and *spring-guns* though probably never intended to annoy such a wanderer as myself, who wished only to enjoy the fine morning air from this eminence.

Thus disappointed in my hopes, I returned to Windsor, much in the same temper and manner as I had yesterday morning from Richmond-Hill, where my wishes had also been frustrated.

When

When I got to my inn, I received from the ill-tempered maid, who feemed to have been ftationed there, on purpofe to plague and vex me, the polite welcome, that on no account fhould I fleep another night there. Luckily, that was not my intention I now write to you in the coffee-room, where two Germans are talking together, who certainly little fufpect, how well I underftand them, if I were to make myfelf known to them, as a German, moft probably, even thefe fellows would not fpeak to me, becaufe I travel on foot. I fancy they are Hanoverians! The weather is fo fine, that notwithftanding the inconveniences I have hitherto experienced on this account, I think, I fhall continue my journey in the fame manner.

OXFORD,

OXFORD, *JUNE* 25.

To what various, singular, and unaccountable fatalities and adventures are not foot-travellers expofed, in this land of carriages and horfes! But, I will begin my relation in form and order.

In Windfor, I was obliged to pay for an old fowl I had for fupper, for a bed-room which I procured with fome difficulty and not without murmurs, and in which, to compleat my mifadventures, I was difturbed by a drunken fellow, and for a couple of diffes of tea, nine fhillings, of which the fowl alone was charged fix fhillings.

As I was going away, the waiter who had ferved me with fo very ill a grace, placed himfelf on the ftairs and faid, " pray remem-" ber the waiter!" I gave him three half-pence: on which he faluted me with the heartieft *G—d d—m you*, fir! I had ever heard. At the door ftood the crofs maid, who alfo accofted me with—" pray, remem-" ber the chamber-maid!" Yes, yes, faid I, I fhall long remember your moft ill-mannered behaviour,

behaviour, and fhameful incivility , and fo I gave her nothing.   I hope fhe was ftung and nettled at my reproof: however fhe ftrove to ftifle her anger by a contemptuous, loud hoife laugh.   Thus, as I left Windfor, I was literally followed by abufe and curfes.

I am very forry to fay, that I rejoiced when I once more perceived the toweis of Windfor behind me.   It is not proper for wanderers to be prowling near the palaces of kings : and fo I fat me down, philofophically, in the fhade of a green hedge, and again iead Milton, no friend of kings, though the fiift of poets. Whatever I may think of their inns, it is im-poffible not to admire and be charmed with this countiy.

I took my way through *Slough* by *Salt-hill*, to *Maidenhead*.   At *Salt-hill*, which can hardly be called even a village, I faw a bar-ber's-fhop , and fo I refolved to get myfelf both fhaved and dreffed.   For putting my hair a little in order, and fhaving me, I was forced to pay him a fhilling.   Oppofite to this fhop, there ftands an elegant houfe, and a neat garden.

Between Salt-hill and Maidenhead, I met
with

with the firft very remarkable and alarming adventure, that has occurred during my pilgrimage.

Hitherto I had fcarcely met a fingle footpaffenger, whilft coaches without number every moment rolled pafs me; for, there are few roads, even in England, more crowded than this weftern road, which leads to Bath and Briftol as well as to Oxford. I now alfo began to meet numbers of people on horfeback; which is by no means an ufual method of travelling.

The road now led me along a low funken piece of ground between high trees, fo that I could not fee far before me, when a fellow in a brown frock and round hat, with a ftick in his hand a great deal ftronger than mine, came up to me. His countenance immediately ftruck me, as having in it fomething fufpicious. He however paffed me; but before I was aware, he turned back and afked me for a halfpenny, to buy, as he faid, fome bread, as he had eat nothing that day I felt in my pocket, and found that I had no halfpence, no, nor even a fixpence, in fhort nothing but fhillings. I told him the circumftance, which I hoped would excufe me: on

which

which he faid with an air and manner, the
drift of which I could not underſtand, "God
"bleſs my ſoul!" this drew my attention
ſtill cloſer to the huge brawny fiſt, which
graſped his ſtick, and that cloſer attention
deteimined me immediately to put my hand
in my pocket and give him a ſhilling. Mean-
while a coach came up. The fellow thanked
me, and went on. Had the coach come a
moment ſooner, I ſhould not eaſily have given
him the ſhilling, which, God knows, I could
not well ſpare. Whether this was a foot-pad
or not, I will not pretend to ſay, but he had
every appearance of it.

I now came to Maidenhead-biidge, which
is five and twenty Engliſh miles fiom
London.

The Engliſh mile-ſtones give me much
pleaſuie, and they certainly are a great convenience to tiavellers. They have often ſeemed to eaſe me of half the diſtance of a journey, merely by telling me how far I had already gone, and by aſſuring me, that I was on
the right road. For, beſides the diſtance from
London, every mile-ſtone informs you, that,
to the next place is ſo many miles : and wheie
there are crofs-roads, there are direction

poſts,

pofts, fo that it is hardly poffible to lofe one's-felf in walking I muft confefs that all this journey has feemed but as it were one continued walk for pleafure.

From Maidenhead-bridge, there is a delightful profpect towards an hill, which extends itfelf along the right bank of the Thames · and on the top of it, there are two beautiful country feats, all furrounded with meadows and parks. The firft is called *Top-low*, and belongs to the earl of Inchiquin; and a little further *Cliefden*, which alfo belongs to him.

Thefe villas feem all to be furrounded with green meadows, lying along thick woods, and, altogether, are moft charming.

From this bridge, it is not far to Maidenhead, near which, on the left, is another profpect of a beautiful feat, belonging to Pennyfton Powney, efq.

All this knowledge I have gained chiefly from my Englifh guide, which I have conftantly in my hand, and in which every thing moft worthy of notice in every mile is marked. Thefe notices I get confirmed or refuted by the people at whofe houfes I ftop; who wonder, how I, who am a Foreigner, have come

come to be fo well acquainted with their
country.

Maidenhead ‑is a place of little note: for
fome mulled ale, which I defiied them to
make me, I was obliged to pay nine-pence.
I fancy they did not here take me to be either
a great, or a very rich, man.   For, I heard
them fay, as I paffed on, " A ftout fellow!"
This, though perhaps not untrue, did not
feem to found in my ears, as very refpectful.

At the end of the village was a fhoe-
maker's fhop; juft as at the end of Salthill,
there was a barber's fhop.

From hence I went to Henley, which is
eleven miles fiom Maidenhead, and thirty-fix
from London.

Having walked pietty faft for fix Englifh
miles together, and being now only five
miles from Henley, I came to a rifing-ground
wheie theie juft happened to be a mile-ftone,
near which I fat down, to enjoy one of the
moft delightful profpects: the contemplation
of which, I recommend to every one, who
may ever happen to come to this fpot. Clofe
before me rofe a foft hill, full of green coin-
fields, fenced with quick-hedges; and at the
top it was encircled with a wood.

At

At some little distance, in a large semi-circle, one green hill rose after another, all around me, gently raising themselves aloft from the banks of the Thames, and on which, woods, meadows, arable lands, and villages, were interspersed in the greatest and most beautiful variety, whilst at their foot, the Thames meandered, in most picturesque windings, among villages, gentlemen's seats, and green vales.

The banks of the Thames are every where beautiful, every where charming: how delighted was I with the sight of it, when, having lost it for a short time, I suddenly and unexpectedly saw it again with all its beautiful banks. In the vale below, flocks were feeding, and from the hills, I heard the sweet chimes of distant bells.

The circumstance that renders these English prospects so enchantingly beautiful, is a concurrence and union of the *tout ensemble*. Every thing coincides and conspires to render them fine, moving, pictures. It is impossible to name, or find a spot, on which the eye would not delight to dwell. Any of the least beautiful of any of these views that I have seen in

H England,

England, would, any where in Germany, be deemed a paradife.

Reinforced, as it were, by this gratifying profpect, to fupport frefh fatigues, I now walked a quick pace, both up and down hills, the five remaining miles to Henley, where I arrived about four in the afternoon.

To the left, juft before I got to Henley, on this fide of the Thames, I faw on a hill, a fine park and a magnificent country-feat, at prefent occupied by general Conway.

Juft before my entrance into Henley, I walked a little directly on the banks of the Thames, and fat myfelf down in the high grafs ; whilft, oppofite to me, on the other fide, lay the park on the hill. As I was a little tired, I fell afleep, and when I awaked the laft rays of the fetting fun juft fhone upon me.

Invigorated by this fweet, though fhort, flumber, I walked on ; and entered the town. It's appearance, however, indicated that it was too fine a place for me, and fo I determined to ftop at an inn on the road-fide ; fuch an one as the Vicar of Wakefield well calls, " the refort of indigence and frugality."

The

The worſt of it was, no one, even in theſe places of refuge, would take me in. Yet, on this road, I met two farmers, the firſt of whom I aſked, whether he thought I could get a night's lodging at an houſe which I ſaw at a diſtance, by the road-ſide. "Yes, ſir, I "dare ſay you may!" he replied. But, he was miſtaken: when I came there, I was accoſted with that ſame harſh ſalutation, which though alas, no longer quite new to me, was ſtill un-pleaſing to my ears. "We have got no "beds; you can't ſtay here to night!" It was the ſame at the other inn, on the road; I was therefore obliged to determine to walk on as far as Nettlebed, which was five miles farther, where I arrived rather late in the evening, when it was indeed quite dark.

Every thing ſeemed to be all alive in this little village; there was a party of militia ſoldiers who were dancing, ſinging, and mak-ing merry. Immediately on my entrance into the village, the firſt houſe that I ſaw, lying on my left was an inn, from which, as uſual in England, a large beam extended acroſs the ſtreet to the oppoſite houſe, from which hung dangling an aſtoniſhing large ſign, with the name of the proprietor.

H 2 "May

" May I ftay here to night?" I afked with
eagernefs : " why, yes, you may ;" an anfwer, which, however cold and furly, made
me exceedingly happy.

They fhewed me into the kitchen, and fet
me down to fup at the fame table with fome
foldiers and the fervants. I now, for the firft
time, found myfelf in one of thofe kitchens
which I had fo often read of in Fielding's
fine novels ; and which certainly give one,
on the whole, a very accurate idea of Englifh
manners.

The chimney in this kitchen, where they
were roafting and boiling, feemed to be taken
off from the reft of the room and enclofed by
a wooden partition · the reft of the apartment was made ufe of as a fitting and eating
room. All round on the fides were fhelves
with pewter difhes and plates, and the ceiling
was well ftored with provifions of various
kinds, fuch as fugar-loaves, black-puddings,
hams, faufages, flitches of bacon, &c.

While I was eating, a poft-chaife drove
up . and in a moment both the folding-doors
were thrown open, and the whole houfe fet in
motion, in order to receive, with all due
refpect, thefe guefts, who, no doubt, were

fuppofed

fuppofed to be perfons of confequence. The gentlemen alighted however only for a moment, and called for nothing but a couple of pots of beer, and then drove away again. Notwithftanding, the people of the houfe behaved to them with all poffible attention, for they came in a poft-chaife.

Though this was only an ordinary village, and they certainly did not take me for a perfon of confequence, they yet gave me a carpeted bed-room, and a very good bed.

The next morning I put on clean linen, which I had along with me, and dreffed myfelf as well as I could. And now, when I thus made my appearance, they did not, as they had the evening before, fhew me into the kitchen, but into the parlour, a room that feemed to be allotted for ftrangers, on the ground-floor. I was alfo now addreffed by the moft refpectful term, *Sir*, whereas, the evening before I had been called only *Mafter*: by this latter appellation, I believe, it is ufual to addrefs only farmers, and quite common people.

This was Sunday, and all the family were in their Sunday-cloaths. I now began to be much pleafed with this village, and fo I re-

H 3   folved

folved to ftop at it for the day, and attend
divine-fervice.   For this purpofe I borrowed
a prayer-book of my hoft.   Mr. *Illing* was his
name, which ftruck me the more, perhaps,
becaufe it is a very common name in Germany.   During my breakfaft, I read over
feveral parts of the Englifh liturgy, and
could not help being ftruck at the circumftance that every word in the whole fervice
feems to be prefcribed and dictated to the
clergyman.   They do not vifit the fick but
by a prefcribed form : as, for inftance, they
muft begin by faying, " Peace be to this
" houfe," &c.

Its being called a *prayer-book*, rather than,
like ours, an *hymn-book*, arifes from the nature of the Englifh fervice, which is compofed very little of finging, and almoft entirely of praying   The pfalms of David,
however, are here tranflated into Englifh
verfe, and are generally printed at the end of
Englifh prayer-books.

The prayer-book, which my landlord lent
me, was quite a family-piece, for all his
children's births and names, and alfo his
own wedding-day, were very carefully fet
down in it.   Even on this account alone
                                              the

the book would not have been uninteresting to me.

At half-past nine, the service began.   Directly opposite to our house, the boys of the village were all drawn up, as if they had been recruits, to be drilled: all well-looking, healthy lads, neat and decently dressed, and with their hair cut short and combed on the forehead, according to the English fashion. Their bosoms were open, and the white frills of their shirts turned back on each side. They seemed to be drawn up here at the entrance of the village, merely to wait the arrival of the clergyman.

I walked a little way out of the village, where, at some distance, I saw several people coming from another village, to attend divine-service here at Nettlebed.

At length came the parson on horseback. The boys pulled of their hats, and all made him very low bows. He appeared to be rather an elderly man, and wore his own hair round and decently dressed, or rather curling naturally.

The bell now rung in, and so I too, with a sort of secret proud sensation, as if I also had been an Englishman, went with my

H 4   prayer-

prayer-book under my arm to church, along with the reft of the congregation; and when I got into the church, the clerk very civilly feated me clofe to the pulpit.

Nothing can poffibly be more fimple, apt, and becoming than the few decorations of this church.

Directly over the altar, on two tables, in large letters, the ten commandments were written. There furely is 'much wifdom and propriety in thus placing, full in the view of the people, the fum and fubftance of all morality.

Under the pulpit, near the fteps that led up to it, was a defk, from which the clergyman read the liturgy. The refponfes were all regularly made by the clerk; the whole congregation joining occafionally, though but in a low voice: As for inftance, the minifter faid, " Lord have mercy upon us !" the clerk and the congregation immediately fub- join, " and forgive us all our fins." In ge- neral, when the clergyman offers up a prayer, the clerk, and the whole congregation anfwer only, *Amen !*

The Englifh fervice muft needs be exceed- ingly fatiguing to the officiating minifter,
inafmuch

inafmuch as, befides a fermon, the greateft part of the liturgy falls to his fhare to read, befides the pfalms, and two leffons. The joining of the whole congregation in prayer has fomething exceedingly folemn and affecting in it. Two foldiers, who fat near me in the church, and who had probably been in London, feemed to wifh to pafs for philofophers, and wits; for they did not join in the prayers of the church.

The fervice was now pretty well advanced, when I obferved fome little ftir in the defk: the clerk was bufy, and they feemed to be preparing for fomething new and folemn; and I alfo perceived feveral mufical inftruments. The clergyman now ftopped and the clerk then faid, in a loud voice, " Let s fing to " the praife and glory of God, the forty- " feventh pfalm."

I cannot well exprefs how affecting and edifying it feemed to me, to hear this whole, orderly, and decent congregation, in this fmall country church, joining together, with vocal and inftrumental mufic, in the praife of their Maker. It was the more grateful, as having been performed not by mercenry muficians, but by the peaceful and pious in-

H 5   habitants,

habitants, of this fweet village. I can hardly figure to myfelf any offering more likely to be grateful to God.

The congregation fang and prayed alternately feveral times, and the tunes of the pfalms were particularly lively and cheerful, though at the fame time fufficiently grave, and uncommonly interefting. I am a warm admirer of all facred mufic, and I cannot but add, that that of the church of England is particularly calculated to raife the heart to devotion. I own it often affected me even to tears.

The clergyman now ftood up and made a fhort, but very proper difcourfe on this text; " Not all they who fay, Lord, Lord! fhall " enter the kingdom of heaven." His language was particularly plain, though forcible; his arguments were no lefs plain, convincing, and earneft, but contained nothing that was particularly ftriking. I do not think the fermon lafted more than half an hour.

This clergyman had not perhaps a very prepoffeffing appearance : I thought him alfo a little diftant and referved, and I did not quite like his returning the bows of the farmers with a very formal nod.

5

I ftaid

I ſtaid till the ſervice was quite over, and then went out of the church with the congregation, and amuſed myſelf with reading the inſcriptions on the tomb-ſtones, in the church-yard, which, in general, are ſimpler, more pathetic, and better written than ours.

There were ſome of them, which, to be ſure, were ludicrous and laughable enough. Among theſe is one on the tomb of a ſmith, which, on account of it's ſingularity, I here copy and ſend you.

> " My ſledge and anvil lie declin'd,
> " My bellows too have loſt their wind ;
> " My fire's extinct, my forge decay'd
> " My coals are ſpent, my iron's gone,
> " My nails are drove, my work is done "

Many of theſe epitaphs cloſed with the following quaint rhymes :

> " Phyſicians were in vain ;
> " God knew the beſt ;
> " So here I reſt "

In the body of the church I ſaw a marble monument of a ſon of the celebrated

H 6   Dr.

Dr. Wallis, with the following fimple and affecting infcription:

" The fame good fenfe which qualified him for every
    " public employment,
" Taught him to fpend his life here in retirement "

All the farmers, whom I faw here, were dreffed, not as ours are, in coarfe frocks, but with fome tafte, in fine good cloth; and were to be diftinguifhed from the people of the town, not fo much by their drefs, as by the greater fimplicity and modefty of their behaviour.

Some foldiers, who probably were ambitious of being thought to know the world, and to be wits, joined me, as I was looking at the church, and feemed to be quite afhamed of it, as, they faid, it was only a very miferable church. On which I took the liberty to inform them, that no church could be miferable, which contained orderly and good people.

I ftaid here to dinner. In the afternoon there was no fervice; the young people, however, went to church, and there fang fome few pfalms. Others of the congregation were

alfo

also prefent.   This was conducted with fo
much decorum, that I could hardly help con-
sidering it, as, actually, a kind of church-
service.   I ftaid, with great pleafure, till this
meeting alfo was over.

I feemed indeed to be enchanted, and as
if I could not leave this village. Three times
did I get off, in order to go on farther, and
as often returned, more than half refolved
to fpend a week, or more, in my favourite
Nettlebed.

But the recollection that I had but a few
weeks to ftay in England, and that I muft
fee Derbyfhire, at length drove me away.
I caft back many *a longing, lingering look* on
the little church-fteeple, and thofe hofpitable
friendly roofs, where, all that morning, I
had found myfelf fo perfectly at home.

It was now nearly three o'clock in the afternoon when I left this place ; and I was ftill
eighteen miles from Oxford.   However, I
feemed refolved to make more than one ftage
of it to Oxford, that feat of the mufes, and
fo, by paffing the night about five miles from
it, to reach it in good time next morning.

The road from Nettlebed feemed to me
but as one long fine gravel-walk in a neat
garden.

·garden. And my pace in it was varied, like that of one walking in a garden. I fometimes walked quick, then flow, and then fat down and read Milton.

When I had got about eight miles from Nettlebed, and was now not far from Dorchefter, I had the Thames at fome diftance on my left, and on the oppofite fide, I faw an extenfive hill, behind which a tall maft feemed to rife. This led me to fuppofe, that on the other fide of the hill there muft needs alfo be a river. The profpect I promifed myfelf from this hill could not poffibly be paffed, and fo I went out of the road to the left over a bridge acrofs the Thames, and mounted the hill, always keeping the maft in view. When I had attained the fummit, I found (and not without fome fhame and much chagrin) that it was all an illufion. There was, in fact, nothing before me but a great plain; and the maft had been fixed there, either as a may-pole only, or to entice curious people out of their way.

I therefore now again, flowly and fullenly, defcended the hill, at the bottom of which was an houfe, where feveral people were looking out of the window, and, as I fuppofed,

laughing

laughing at me. Even if it were fo, it feemed to be but fair, and fo it rather amufed, than vexed, me; and I continued to jog on, without much regreting my wafte journey to the maft.

Not far from Dorchefter, I had another delightful view. The country here became fo fine, that I pofitively could not prevail on myfelf to quit it, and fo I laid myfelf down on the green turf, which was fo frefh and fweet, that I could almoft have been contented, like Nebuchadnezzar, to have grazed on it. The moon was at the full, the fun darted its laft parting rays through the green hedges; to all which was added, the overpowering fragrance of the meadows, the diverfified fong of the birds, the hills that fkirted the Thames; fome of them of a light, and others of a dark-green hue, with the tufted tops of trees difperfed here and there among them. The contemplation of all thefe delightful circumftances well-nigh overcame me.

I arrived rather late at Dorchefter. This is only a fmall place, but there is in it a large and noble old church. As I was walking along, I faw feveral ladies, with their heads dreffed, leaning out of their windows, or ftanding before the houfes;

houfes; and this made me conclude, that this was too fine a place for me, and fo I determined to walk on three quarters of a mile farther to Nuneham; which place is only five miles from Oxford. When I reached Nuneham, I was not a little tired; and it was alfo quite dark.

The place confifts of two rows of low, neat houfes, built clofe to each other, and as regular and uniform as a London ftreet. All the doors feemed to be fhut, and even a light was to be feen only in a few of them.

At length quite at the end of the place, I perceived a great fign hanging acrofs the ftreet, and the laft houfe to the left was the inn, at which every thing feemed to be ftill in motion.

I entered without ceremony, and told them my errand, which was, that I intended to fleep there that night. "By no means!" was the anfwer, "it was utterly impoffible; "the whole houfe was full, and all their beds "engaged, and, as I had come fo far, I might "even as well walk on the remaining five "miles to Oxford."

Being very hungry, I requefted that, at leaft, they would give me fomething to

eat,

eat. To this they anfwered, that, as I could not ftay all night there, it would be more proper for me to fup where I lodged, and fo I might go on.

At length, quite humbled by the untoward-nefs of my circumftances, I afked for a pot of beer, and that they did vouchfafe to give me, for ready money only. but a bit of bread, to eat with it (for which alfo I would willingly have paid) they peremptorily refufed me.

Such unparallelled inhofpitality I really could not have expected in an Englifh inn. but, re-folving, with a kind of fpiteful indignation, to fee how far their inhumanity would carry them, I begged that they would only let me fleep on a bench, and merely give me houfe-room, adding, that if they would grant me that boon only, I would pay them the fame as for a bed, for, that I was fo tired, I could not poffibly go any father. Even in the mo-ment that I was thus humbly foliciting this humble boon, they banged the door to full in my face.

As here, in a fmall village, they had re-fufed to receive me, it feemed to be pre-fumption to hope, that I fhould gain ad-mittance at Oxford. What could I do? I

was

was much tired, and fo as it was not a very cold night, I refolved to pafs it in the open air; in this refolution, bouncing from this rude inn, I went to look out for a convenient fpot for that purpofe, in an adjoining field, beneath fome friendly tree. Juft as I had found a place, which I thought would do, and was going to pull off my great coat, to lay under my head, by way of pillow, I heard fome one behind me, following me with a quick pace. At firft, I was alarmed, but my fears were foon difpelled by his calling after me, and afking, " if I would accept of company."

As little as any one is to be trufted, who thus follows you into a field in a dark night, yet it was a pleafure to me to find that there were ftill fome beings not quite inhuman; and at leaft one perfon, who ftill interefted himfelf about me: I therefore ftopped, and as he came up to me, he faid that if I was a good walker, we might keep each other company, as he was alfo going to Oxford. I readily accepted of his propofal, and fo we immediately fet off together.

Now, as I could not tell whether my travelling companion was to be trufted or not, I foon took an opportunity to let him know that

I was

I was poor, and much diftreffed. To confirm this, I told him of the inhumanity with which I had juft been treated at the inn; where they refufed a poor wanderer fo much as a place to to lay his head, or even a morfel of bread for his money.

My companion fomewhat excufed the people, by faying, that the houfe was really full of people who had been at work in the neighbourhood, and now flept there. But that they had refufed me a bit of bread, he certainly could not juftify. As we went along, other topics of converfation were ftarted, and among other things, he afked me where I came from that day?

I anfwered, from Nettlebed, and added, that I had attended divine fervice there that morning.

As you probably paffed through Dorchefter, this afternoon, faid he, you might have heard me preach alfo, had you come into the church there, for that is my curacy from which I am juft come, and am now returning to Oxford. So you are a clergyman, faid I, quite overjoyed that, in a dark night, I had met a companion on the road, who was of the fame profeffion as myfelf. And I alfo, faid I, am a preacher of the gofpel, though not of this country. And now, I thought it right to

give

give him to underſtand that it was not, as I had before intimated, out of abſolute poverty, but with a view of becoming better acquainted with men and manners, that I thus travelled on foot.   He was as much pleaſed with this agreeable meeting as myſelf, and before we took a ſtep farther, we cordially ſhook hands.

He now began to addreſs me in Latin, and on my anſwering him in that language, which I attempted to pronounce according to the Engliſh manner of ſpeaking it, he applauded me not a little for my correct pronunciation. He then told me, that ſome years ago, in the night alſo, and nearly at the ſame ſpot where he found me, he had met another German, who likewiſe ſpoke to him in Latin; but this unknown countryman of mine had pronounced it ſo very badly, that he ſaid, it was abſolutely unintelligible.

The converſation now turned on various theological matters, and among others on the novel notions of a Dr. Prieſtly, whom he roundly blamed.   I was not at all diſpoſed to diſpute that point with him, and ſo, profeſſing with great ſincerity, an high eſteem for the Church of England, and great reſpect and regard for its clergy, I ſeemed to gain his good opinion.

Beguiling

Beguiling the tedioufnefs of the road by fuch difcourfe, we were now got, almoft without knowing it, quite to Oxford.

He told me, I fhould now fee one of the fineft, and moft beautiful cities, not only in England, but in all Europe. All he lamented was, that, on account of the darknefs of the night, I fhould not immediately fee it.

This really was the cafe, and now, faid he, as we entered the town, I introduce you into Oxford, by one of the fineft, the longeft, and moft beautiful ftreets, not only in this city, but in England, and I may fafely add, in all Europe.

The beauty and the magnificence of the ftreet I could not diftinguifh, but of its length I was perfectly fenfible by my fatigue, for, we ftill went on, and ftill through the longeft, the fineft, and moft beautiful ftreet in Europe, which feemed to have no end, nor had I any affurance that I fhould be able to find a bed for myfelf in all this famous ftreet. At length my companion ftopped to take leave of me, and faid, he fhould now go to his college.

And I, faid I, will feat myfelf for the night on this ftone-bench, and await the morning,

as

as it will be in vain for me, I imagine, to look for shelter in an house at this time of night.

Seat yourself on a stone, said my companion, and shook his head : No! no! come along with me to a neighbouring ale-house, where, it is possible, they mayn't be gone to bed, and we may yet find company. We went on, a few houses further, and then knocked at a door It was then nearly twelve. They readily let us in , but how great was my astonishment, when, on our being shewn into a room on the left, I saw a great number of clergymen, all with their gowns and bands on, sitting round a large table, each with his pot of beer before him. My travelling companion introduced me to them, as a German clergyman, whom he could not sufficiently praise, for my correct pronunciation of the Latin, my orthodoxy, and my good walking.

I now saw myself, in a moment as it were, all at once transported into the midst of a company, all apparently, very respectable men, but all strangers to me. And it appeared to me extraordinary, that I should, thus at midnight, be in Oxford, in a large company

pany

pany of Oxonian clergy, without well knowing how I had got there.   Mean-while, how.
ever, I took all the pains in my power to recommend myfelf to my company, and, in
the courfe of converfation, I gave them as
good an account as I could of our German
Univerfities, neither denying, nor conceal-
ing, that, now and then, we had riots and
difturbances. "O we are very unruly here
too," faid one of the clergymen, as he took
a hearty draught out of his pot of beer, and
knocked on the table with his hand.   The
converfation now became louder, more general, and a little confufed: they enquired
after Mr. Bruns, at prefent Profeffor at
Helmftadt, and who was known by many of
them.

Among thefe gentlemen, there was one of
the name of *Clerk*, who feemed ambitious to
pafs for a great wit, which he attempted, by
ftarting fundry objections to the Bible.   I
fhould have liked him better if he had confined himfelf to punning and playing on his
own name, by telling us, again and again,
that he fhould ftill be, at leaft, a *Clerk*, even
though he fhould never become a *clergyman*.
Upon the whole, however, he was, in his
way,

way, a man of some humour, and an agreeable companion.

Among other objections, to the Scriptures, he started this one to my travelling companion, whose name I now learnt was *Maud*, that it was said, in the Bible, that God was a *wine-bibber*, and a *drunkard*. On this Mr. Maud fell into a violent passion, and maintained that it was utterly impossible that any such passage should be found in the Bible. Another Divine, a *Mr. Caern*, referred us to his absent brother, who had already been forty years in the church, and must certainly know something of such a passage, if it were in the Bible, but he would venture to lay any wager his brother knew nothing of it.

Waiter! fetch a Bible! called out Mr. Clerk, and a great family Bible was immediately brought in, and opened on the table, among all the beer jugs.

Mr. Clerk turned over a few leaves, and in the Book of Judges, 9th chapter, verse xiii, he read, " Should I leave my wine, which " cheareth God and man ?"

Mr. Maud and Mr. Caern, who had before been most violent, now sat as if struck dumb. A silence of some minutes prevailed, when, all

a£

at once, the fpirit of revelation feemed to come on me, and I faid, " Why, gentlemen! " you muft be fenfible, that is but an allego- " rical expreffion: and I added, how often, " in the Bible, are Kings called Gods!"

" Why, yes, to be fure," faid Mr. Maud and Mr Caern, it is an allegorical expreffion; nothing can be more clear, it is a metaphor, and therefore it is abfurd to underftand it in a literal fenfe. And now they, in their turn, triumphed over poor *Clerk*, and drank large draughts to my health. Mr. *Clerk*, however, had not yet exhaufted his quiver, and fo he defired them to explain to him a paffage in the Prophecy of Ifaiah, where it is faid, in ex-prefs terms, that *God is a barber*. Mr. Maud was fo enraged at this, that he called *Clerk* an impudent fellow, and Mr. *Caern* again ftill more earneftly referred us to his brother, who had been forty years in the church, and who, therefore, he doubted not, would alfo confider Mr. Clerk as an impudent fellow, if he maintained any fuch abominable notions. Mr. Clerk, all this while, fat per-fectly compofed, without either a fmile or a frown; but turning to a paffage in Ifaiah, chapter vii. v. 20, he read thefe words:—" In " the

I

" the fame day, the Lord fhall fhave with a
" razor—the head, and the hair of the feet;
" and it fhall alfo confume the beard." If Mr.
Maud and Mr. Caern were before ftunned
and confounded, they were much more fo
now, and even Mr. Caern's brother, who
had been forty years in the church, feemed
to have left them in the lurch! for he was no
longer referred to.   I broke filence a fecond
time and faid· Why, gentlemen, this alfo is
clearly metaphorical, and it is equally juft,
ftrong, and beautiful.   " Aye, to be fure it
is," rejoined Mr Maud and Mr. Caern, both
in a breath, at the fame time, rapping the
table with their knuckles.   I went on, and
faid; you know it was the cuftom for thofe
who were captives to have their beards fhorn;
the plain import, then, of this remarkable
expreffion is nothing more, than that God
would deliver the rebellious Jews to be pri-
foners to a foreign people, who would fhave
their beards! Ay to be fure it is, any body may
fee it is; why it is as clear as the day! fo it is,
rejoined Mr. Caern, and my brother, who
has been forty years in the church, explains
it juft as this gentleman does.

We had now gained a fecond victory over
                                                    Mr.

Mr. Clerk; who, being, perhaps, afhamed either of himfelf, or of us, now remained quiet, and made no further objections to the Bible. My health, however, was again *encored,* and drank in ftrong ale; which as my company feemed to like fo much, I was forry I could not like. It either intoxicated, or ftupified me, and I do think it overpowers one much fooner than fo much wine would. The converfation now turned on many other different fubjects. At laft, when morning drew near, Mr. Maud fuddenly exclaimed, d——n me, I muft read prayers this morning at All-Soul's! *D——n me* is an abbreviation of G—d d——n me, which, in England, does not feem to mean more mifchief, or harm, than any of our, or their, common expletives in converfation, fuch as *O gemini! or the Duce take me!*

Before Mr. Maud went away, he invited me to go and fee him in the morning; and very politely offered himfelf to fhew me the curiofities of Oxford. The reft of the company now alfo difperfed; and as I had once (though in fo fingular a manner) been introduced into fo reputable a fociety, the people of the houfe made no difficulty of giving me lodging, but, with great civility, fhewed me a very decent bed-chamber.

I am

I am almoſt aſhamed to own that, next morning, when I awoke, I had got ſo dreadful an head-ach, fiom the copious and numerous toaſts of my jolly and reverend friends, that I could not poſſibly get up, ſtill leſs could I wait on Mi Maud at his College.

The inn where I was, goes by the name of *The Mitre*. Compaied to Windſor, I theie found Prince-like attendance. Being, perhaps, a little elevated, the preceding evening, I had, in the gaiety, oi perhaps, in the vanity of my heart, told the waiter, that he muſt not think, becauſe I came on foot, that therefore I ſhould give him leſs than others gave. I aſſured him of the contraiy. It was probably not a little owing to this aſſurance, that I had ſo much attention ſhewn to me.

I now determined to ſtay at leaſt a couple of days at Oxford, it was neceſſary and proper, if for no other reaſon, yet merely that I might have clean linen. No people are ſo cleanly as the Engliſh, nor ſo particular about neat and clean linen. For, one afternoon, my ſhirt not having been lately changed, as I was walking through a little ſtreet, I heaid two women, who were ſtanding at a door, call after me, " look at the gentleman there ! A

" fine

" fine gentleman indeed, who cannot afford
" even a clean shirt!"

I dined below with the family, and a few
other persons, and the conversation, in general, was agreeable enough.   I was obliged
to tell them many wonderful stories (for, who
are so illiterate, or insensible, as not to be
delighted with the marvellous!) concerning
Germany, and the King of Prussia.   They
could not sufficiently admire my courage in
determining to travel on foot, although they
could not help approving of the motive.   At
length, however, it came out, and they can-
didly owned, that I should not have been received into their house, had I not been introduced as I was.

I was now confirmed in my suspicions, that,
in England, any person undertaking so long a
journey on foot, is sure to be looked upon, and
considered as either a beggar, or a vagabond, or
some necessitous wretch, which is a character
not much more popular than that of a rogue;
so that I could now easily account for my reception in Windsor, and at Nuneham.   But,
with all my partiality for this country, it is
impossible, even in theory, and much less so
in practice, to approve of a system which

confines

confines all the pleafures and benefits of travel to the rich. A poor peripatetic is hardly allowed even the humble merit of being honeft.

As I ftill intended to purfue my journey to Derbyfhire, I was advifed (at leaft till I got further into the country) to take a place in a poft-coach. They told me, that the further I got from London, the more reafonable and humble I fhould find the people; every thing would be cheaper; and every body more hofpitable. This determined me to go, in the poft-coach, from Oxford to Birmingham; where Mr. Pointer, of London, had recommended me to a Mr. Fothergill, a merchant there, and from thence to continue my journey on foot.

Monday I fpent at Oxford, but rather unpleafantly, on account of my head-ach. Mr. Maud himfelf came to fetch me, as he had promifed he would, but I found myfelf unable to go with him.

Notwithftanding this, in the afternoon, I took a little walk up an hill, which lies to the north of Oxford; and from the top of which I could-fee the whole city, which did not, however, appear to me nearly fo beautiful and magnificent

magnificent as Mr Maud had defcribed it to me during our laft night's walk.

The Colleges are moftly in the gothic tafte, and much overloaded with ornaments, and built with grey ftone, which, perhaps, while it is new, looks pretty well, but it has now the moft dingy, dirty, and difgufting appearance, that you can poffibly imagine.

Only one of thefe Colleges is in the modern ftile. The houfes of the city are in general ordinary, in fome parts quite miferable, in fome ftreets they are only one ftory high, and have fhingled roofs. To me Oxford feemed to have but a dull and gloomy look, and I cannot but wonder how it ever came to be confidered as fo fine a city, and next to London.

I remained on the hill, on which there was a flight of fteps that led to a fubterraneous walk, till fun-fet, and faw feveral ftudents walking here, who wore their black gowns over their coloured cloaths, and flat fquare hats, juft like thofe I had feen worn by the Eton fcholars. This is the general drefs of all thofe who belong to the Univerfities, with the exception of a very trifling difference, by which perfons of high birth and rank are diftinguifhed.

It

It is probably on account of thefe gowns, that the Members of the Univerfity are called *Gownfmen*, to diftinguifh them from the citizens who are called *Townfmen*, and when you want to mention all the inhabitants of Oxford together, you fay, "the whole town, Gownf- "men and Townfmen."

This drefs, I muft own, pleafes me far beyond the boots, cockades, and other flippery, of many of our ftudents.   Nor am I lefs delighted with the better behaviour and conduct which, in general, does fo much credit to the Students of Oxford.

The next morning Mr. Maud, according to his promife, fhewed me fome of the things moft worthy of notice in Oxford.   And firft he took me to his own room in his own College, which was on the ground floor, very low, and dark, and refembled a cell, at leaft as much as a place of ftudy.   The name of this College, is *Corpus Chrifti*.   He next conducted me to *All Souls College*, a very elegant building, in which the chapel is particularly beautiful.   Mr. Maud alfo fhewed me, over the altar here, a fine painting of Mengs, at the fight of which, he fhewed far more fenfibility than I thought him poffeffed of.   He

faid,

said, that notwithstanding he saw that painting almost daily, he never saw it without be--
ing much affected.

This painting represented Mary Magda-
len, when she first suddenly sees Jesus standing before her, and falls at his feet.   And,
in her countenance, pain, joy, grief, in short
almost all the strongest of our passions, are
expressed in so masterly a manner, that no
man of true taste was ever tired of contemplating it;   the longer it is looked at, the
more it is admired.   He now also shewed me
the library of this College, which is provided with a gallery round the top, and the
whole is most admirably regulated and ar-
ranged.   Among other things, I here saw a
description of Oxford, with plates to illustrate
it : and I cannot help observing what, though
trite, is true, that all these places look much
better, and are far more beautiful on paper,
than they appeared to me to be, as I looked
at them, where they actually stand.

Afterwards Mr Maud conducted me to the
Bodleian library, which is not unworthy of being compared to the *Vatican* at Rome ; and
next to the building, which is called the
Theatre, and where the public orations are de-
lvered.

I 5

livered. This is a circular building with a gallery all round it, which is furnished with benches one above the other, on which the Doctors, Masters of Arts, and Students sit, and directly opposite to each other are erected two chairs, or pulpits, from which the disputants harangue and contend.

Chrst Church and *Queen's College* are the most modern, and, I think, indisputably the best built of all the Colleges. Baliol College seems particularly to be distinguished on account of its antiquity, and its complete gothic stile of building.

Mr. Maud told me that a good deal of money might be sometimes earned by preaching at Oxford, for all the Members of a certain standing are obliged, in their turn, to preach in the Church of the University; but many of them, when it comes to their turn, prefer the procuring a substitute, and so not unfrequently, pay as high as five or six guineas for a sermon.

Mr. Maud also told me he had been now eighteen years at this University, and might be made a Doctor, whenever he chose it, he was a Master of Arts, and according to his own account gave lectures in his College on

the

the Claffics.   He alfo did the duty, and officiated as curate, occafionally, in fome of the
neighbouring villages.   Going along the
ftreet, we met the Englifh Poet Laureat,
Warton, now rather an elderly man; and yet
he is ftill the Fellow of a College. His greateft
pleafure, next to poetry, is, as Mr. Maud told
me, fhooting wild ducks.

Mr. Maud, feemed upon the whole, to be
a moft worthy and philanthropic man.   He
told me that where he now officiated, the
clerk was dead, and had left a numerous family, in the greateft diftrefs, and that he was
going to the place, next day, on purpofe to try
if he could bring about the election of the fon,
a lad of about fixteen years of age, in the place
of his deceafed father, as clerk, to fupport a
neceffitous family.

At *The Mitre*, the inn where I lodged,
there was hardly a minute, in which fome
ftudents, or others, did not call, either to
drink, or to amufe themfelves in converfation
with the daughter of the landlord, who is not
only handfome, but fenfible, and well-behaved.

They often fpoke to me much in praife of
a German, of the name of *Mitchel*, at leaft
they pronounced it fo, who had for many

N 6   years

years rendered himself famous as a musician. I was rejoiced to hear one of my countrymen thus praised by the English; and wished to have paid him a visit, but I had not the good fortune to find him at home.

CASTLETON,

CASTLETON, JUNE 30TH.

BEFORE I tell you any thing of the place where I now am, I will proceed regularly in my narrative, and so begin now, where I left off in my last letter. On Tuesday afternoon Mr. Maud took me to the different walks about Oxford, and often remarked, that they were not only the finest in England, but, he believed, in Europe. I own, I do not think, he over rated their merit. There is one, in particular near the river, and close to some charming meadows, behind *Corpus Christi* College, which may fairly challenge the world.

We here seated ourselves on a bench, and Mr Maud drew a review from his pocket, where, among other things, a German book of Professor Beckman's was reviewed, and applauded. Mr Maud seemed, on this occasion, to shew some respect for German literature. At length we parted. He went to fill up the vacancy of the clerk's place at Dorchester, and I to the Mitre, to prepare for my departure from Oxford, which took place on Wednesday morning at three o'clock, in the

the poſt-coach. Confidering the pleaſing, if not kind, attention ſhewn me here, I own, I thought my bill not unreaſonable; though to be ſure, it made a great hole in my little purſe.

Within this coach there was another young man, who, though dreſſed in black, yet to judge from the cockade in his hat might be an officer. The outſide was quite full, with ſoldiers and their wives. The women of the lower claſs here, wear a kind of ſhort cloak made of red cloth, but women in general, from the higheſt to the loweſt, wear hats, which differ from each other leſs in faſhion, than they do in fineneſs.

Faſhion is ſo generally attended to among the Engliſh women, that the pooreſt maid ſervant, is careful to be in the faſhion. They ſeem to be particularly ſo, in their hats, or bonnets, which they all wear: and they are in my opinion far more becoming than the very unſightly hoods and caps which our Ger-men women, of the rank of citizens, wear. There is, through all ranks here, not near ſo great a diſtinction between high and low, as there is in Germany.

I had,

I had, during this day, a little head ach; which rendered me more silent and referved to my company, then is either ufual in England, or natural to me. The English are taxed, perhaps too haftily, with being fhy and diftant to ftrangers. I do not think this was, even formerly, their true character; or that any fuch fentiment is conveyed in Virgil's *" Hofpitibus feros."* Be this as it may, the cafe was here reverfed. The Englishman here fpoke to me feveral times in a very friendly manner, while I teftified not the leaft inclination to enter into converfation with him.

He however owned afterwards, that it was this very apparent referve of mine, that firft gained me his good opinion.

He faid, he had ftudied phyfic, but with no immediate view of practifing it. His intention, he faid, was to go to the Eaft Indies; and there, firft, to try his fortune as an officer. And he was now going to Birmingham, merely to take leave of his three fifters, whom he much loved, and who were at fchool there.

I endeavoured to merit his confidence by telling him, in my turn, of my Journey on foot through England; and by relating to him

him a few of the moſt remarkable of my adventures, he frankly told me, he thought, it was venturing a great deal; yet he applauded the deſign of my journey, and did not ſeverely cenſure my plan. On my aſking him, why Engliſhmen, who were ſo remarkable for acting up to their own notions and ideas, did not, now and then, merely to ſee life in every point of view, travel on foot: O, ſaid he, we are too rich, too lazy, and too proud.

And, moſt true it is, that the pooreſt Engliſhman one ſees, is prouder and better pleaſed to expoſe himſelf to the danger of having his neck broken, on the outſide of a ſtage, than to walk any conſiderable diſtance, though he might walk ever ſo much at his eaſe. I own, i was frightened and diſtreſſed, when I ſaw the women, when we occaſionally ſtopped, get down from the top of the coach. One of them was actually once in much danger of a terrible fall from the roof, becauſe, juſt as ſhe was going to alight, the horſes all at once unexpectedly went on. From Oxford to Birmingham is ſixty two miles. But all that was to be ſeen between the two places was entirely loſt to me, for I was again

mewed

mewed up in a poft-coach, and driven along with fuch velocity from one place to another, that I feemed to myfelf as doing nothing lefs than travelling.

My companion however made me amends, in fome meafure, for this lofs. He feemed to be an exceedingly good tempered and intelligent man; and I felt, in this fhort time, a prepoffeffion in his favor, one does not eafily form for an ordinary perfon. This, I flattered myfelf, was alfo the cafe with him, and it would mortify me not a little to think he had quite forgotten me, as I am fure I fhall never forget him.

Juft as we had been fome time eagerly converfing about Shakefpeare, we arrived, without either of us having thought of it, at Stratford upon Avon, Shakefpeare's birth place, where our coach ftopped, that being the end of one ftage. We were ftill two and twenty miles from Birmingham, and ninety four from London. I need not tell you, what our feelings were, on thus fetting our feet on claffic ground.

It was here that, perhaps, the greateft genius nature ever produced, was born. Here he firft lifp'd his native tongue, here firft conceived

ceived the embrios of thofe compofitions
which were afterwards to-charm a liftening
world; and on thefe plains, the young *Her-*
cules firft played. And here too, in this
lowly hut, with a few friends, he happily
fpent the decline of his life, after having retired from the great theatre of that bufy
world, whofe manners he had fo faithfully
pourtrayed.

The River Avon is here pretty broad, and
a row of neat, though humble, cottages, only
one ftory high, with fhingled roofs, are
ranged all along its banks. Thefe houfes im-
preffed me ftrongly with the idea of patriarchal fimplicity and content.

We went to fee Shakefpeare's own houfe;
which, of all the houfes at Stratford, I think
is now the worft; and one that made the
leaft appearance. Yet, who would not be
proud to be the owner of it? There now
however lived in it only two old people, who
fhew it to ftrangers for a trifle, and what
little they earn thus, is their chief income.

Shakefpeare's chair, in which he ufed to fit
before the door, was fo cut to pieces that it
hardly looked like a chair, for every one that
travels through Stratford, cuts off a chip, as

a rea remembrance which he carefully preserves, and deems a precious relique.   I also cut myself a piece of it, but, reverencing Shakespeare as I do, I am almoſt aſhamed to own to you, it was ſo ſmall that I have loſt it, and therefore you will not ſee it on my return.

As we travelled, I obſerved every ſpot with attention, fancying to myſelf, that ſuch or ſuch a ſpot might be the place where ſuch a genius as Shakeſpeare's firſt dawned, and received thoſe firſt impreſſions from ſurrounding nature, which are ſo ſtrongly marked in all his works.   The firſt impreſſions of childhood, I knew, were ſtrong, and permanent: of courſe, I made ſure of ſeeing, here, ſome images at leaſt of the wonderful conceptions of this wonderful man.   But my imagination miſled me, and I was diſappointed, for I ſaw nothing in the country thereabouts, at all ſtriking, or, in any reſpect, particularly beautiful.   It was not at all wild and romantic, but rather diſtinguiſhed for an air of neatneſs and ſimplicity

We arrived at Birmingham about three o'clock in the afternoon.   I had already paid ſixteen ſhillings at Stratford, for my place in the coach from Oxford to Birmingham.

At

At Oxford, they had not afked any thing of me : and indeed you are not obliged in general, in England, as you are in Germany, to pay your paffage before hand.

- My companion and myfelf alighted at the inn where the coach ftopped. We parted with fome reluctance, and I was obliged to promife him, that, on my return to London, I would certainly call on him: for which purpofe he gave me his addrefs. His father was Dr Wilfon; a celebrated author in his particular ftile of writing.

I now enquired for the houfe of Mr Fothergill, to whom I was recommended, and I was readily directed to it, but had the misfortune to learn, at the fame time, that this very Mr. Fothergill had died about eight days before. As, therefore, under thefe circumftances my recommendation to him was likely to be of but little ufe, I had the lefs defire to tarry long at Birmingham: And fo, without ftaying a minute longer, I immediately enquired the road to Derby; and left Birmingham. Of this famous manufacturing town, therefore, I can give you no account

The road from Birmingham onwards is not very agreeable, being, in general, uncommonly

monly fandy. Yet, the fame evening, I reached a little place called *Sutton*, where every thing however appeared to be too grand for me to hope to obtain lodgings in it: till, quite at the end of it, I came to a fmall inn, with the fign of *the Swan*, under which was written *Aulton, Brick-maker*.

This feemed to have fomething in it that fuited me, and therefore I boldly went into it: and when in, I did not immediately, as heretofore, enquire if I could ftay all night there, but afked for a pint of ale. I own, I felt myfelf difheartened, by their calling me nothing but *Mafter*, and by their fhewing me into the kitchen, where the landlady was fitting at a table, and complaining much of the tooth-ach. The compaffion I expreffed for her on this account, as a ftranger, feemed foon to recommend me to her favour, and fhe herfelf afked me, if I would not ftay the night there? To this I moft readily affented, and thus, I was again happy in a lodging for another night.

The company I here met with, confifted of a female chimney-fweeper and her children; who, on my fitting down in the kitchen, foon

2

drank

drank to my health, and began a converfation with me and the landlady.

She related to us her hiftory, which, I am not afhamed to own, I thought not uninterefting. She had married early, but had the hard luck to be foon deprived of her hufband, by his being preffed as a foldier. She neither faw, nor heard of him for many years; and fo concluded he was dead. Thus deftitute, fhe lived feven years as a fervant in Ireland, without any one's knowing that fhe was married. During this time her hufband, who was a chimney-fweeper, came back to England, and fettled at Litchfield, refumed his old trade and did well in it. As foon as he was in good circumftances he every where made enquiry for his wife, and at laft found out where fhe was, and immediately fetched her from Ireland. There furely is fomething pleafing in this conftancy of affection in a chimney-fweeper. She told us, with tears in her eyes, in what a ftile of grandeur he had conducted her into Litchfield; and how, in honour to her, he made a fplendid feaft on the occafion. At this fame Litchfield, which is only two miles from Sutton, and through which fhe faid the road lay, which I was to

travel

travel to-morrow, fhe ftill lived with this fame excellent hufband, where they were noted for their induftry; where every body refpected them, and where, though in the loweft fphere, they are paffing through life, neither ufelefsly, nor unhappily.

The landlady, during her abfence, told me, as in confidence, that this chimney-fweeper's hufband, as meanly as I might fancy fhe now appeared, was worth a thoufand pounds, and that, without reckoning in their plate and furniture: that he always wore his filver watch, and that when he paffed through Sutton, and lodged there, he paid like a nobleman.

She further remarked, that the wife was indeed rather low-lived, but that the hufband was one of the beft-behaved, politeft and civileft men in the world. I had, myfelf, taken notice, that this fame dingy companion of mine had fomething fingularly coarfe and vulgar, in her pronunciation. The word *old*, for example, fhe founded like *auld*. In other refpects, I had not yet remarked any ftriking variety or difference from the pronunciation of Oxford, or London.

To-

To-morrow the chimney-sweeper, said she, her husband, would not be at home, but if I came back by the way of Litchfield, she would take the liberty to request the honour of a visit, and to this end, she told me her name, and the place of her abode.

At night the rest of the family, a son and daughter of the landlady, came home, and paid all possible attention to their sick mother. I supped with the family, and they here behaved to me, as if we had already lived many years together.

Happening to mention, that I was, if not a scholar, yet a student, the son told me, there was at Sutton a celebrated Grammar School, where the school-master received two hundred pounds a year settled salary, besides the income arising from the scholars. And this was only in a village. I thought, and not without some shame and sorrow, of our Grammar Schools in Germany, and the miserable pay of the masters.

When I paid my reckoning the next morning, I observed the uncommon difference here and at Windsor, Nettlebed, and Oxford. At Oxford I was obliged to pay for my supper, bed and breakfast, at least three shillings, and

one

one to the waiter. I here paid for my fupper, bed and breakfaft, only one fhilling, and to the daughter, whom I was to confider as chambermaid, fourpence; for which fhe very civilly thanked me, and gave me a written recommendation to an Inn at Litchfield, where I fhould be well lodged, as the people in Litchfield were, in general, fhe faid, very proud. This written recommendation was a mafter-piece of orthography, and fhewed that, in England, as well as elfewhere, there are people who write entirely from the ear, and as they pronounce. In Englifh, however, it feems to look particularly odd. but perhaps, that may be the cafe in all languages that are not native.

I took leave here as one does of good friends, with a certain promife, that on my return I would certainly call on them again.

At noon I got to Litchfield: an old fafhioned town, with narrow dirty ftreets, where, for the firft time, I faw round panes of glafs in the windows. The place, to me, wore an unfriendly appearance; I therefore made no ufe of my recommendation, but went ftraight through, and only bought fome bread at a baker's, which I took along with me.

K   At

At night I reached Burton, where the famous Burton Ale is brewed. By this time, I felt myself pretty well tired, and therefore proposed to stay the night here. But my courage failed me, and I dropped the resolution, immediately on my entering the town. The houses, and every thing else seemed to wear as grand an appearance, almost, as if I had been still in London. And yet the manners of some of its inhabitants were so thoroughly rustic, and rude, that I saw them actually pointing at me with their fingers, as a foreigner. And now, to compleat my chagrin and mortification, I came to a long street, where every body, on both sides of the way, were at their doors, and actually made me run the gauntlet through their inquiring looks. Some even hissed at me, as I passed along. All my arguments, to induce me to pluck up my courage, such as the certainty that I should never see these people again, nor they me, were of no use: Burton became odious and almost insupportable to me, and the street appeared as long, and tired me as much, as if I had walked a mile. This strongly marked contemptuous treatment of a stranger, who was travelling through their coun-

try,

tiy, merely from the refpect he bore it, I experienced no where but at Burton.

How happy did I feel when I again found myfelf out of their town; although at that moment I did not know where I fhould find a lodging for the night, and was, befides, exceffively tired.   But I purfued my journey and ftill kept in the road to Derby along a foot path which I knew to be right.   It led acrofs a very pleafant mead, the hedges of which were fepaiated by ftiles, over which I was often obliged to clamber.   When I had walked fome diftance, without meeting with an inn on the road, and it already began to be daik, I at laft fat me down, near a fmall *toll-houfe*, or a turnpike-gate, in oider to reft myfelf, and alfo to fee whether the man at the turnpike, could and would lodge me.

Aftei I had fat heie a confiderable time, a faimer came riding by, and afked me wheic I wanted to go? I told him I was fo tired that I could go no faithei. On this the good natui'd, and truly hofpitable man, of his own accord, and without the leaft diftiuft, offeied to take me behind him on his horfe, and caiiy me to a neighbouring inn, where, he faid, I might ftay all night.

K 2   The

The horse was a tall one, and I could not easily get up. The turnpikeman, who appeared to be quite deciepid and infirm, on this came out. I took it for granted, however, that he who appeared to have hardly sufficient strength to support himself, could not help me. This poor looking, feeble, old man, however, took hold of me with one arm, and lifted me with a single jirk upon the horse, so quick and so alertly, that it quite astonished me.

And now I trotted on with my charming farmer, who did not ask me one single impertinent question, but set me down quietly at the inn, and immediately rode away to his own village, which lay to the left.

This inn was called *the bear*, and not improperly: for the landlord went about, and growled at his people just like a bear, so that at first I expected no favourable reception. I endeavoured to gentle him a little by asking for a mug of ale, and once or twice drinking to him. This succeeded; he soon became so very civil and conversable, that I began to think him quite a pleasant fellow. This device I had learnt of the Vicar of Wakefield, who always made his hosts affable, by inviting

them

them to drink with him It was an expedient that suited me also in another point of view, as the strong ale of England did not at all agree with me.

This innkeeper called me, *Sir*, and he made his people lay a separate table for himself, and me, for, he said, he could see plainly, I was a gentleman.

In our chat, we talked much of George the second, who appeared to be his favourite king, much more so than George the third.   And among other things, we talked of the battle at Dettingen, of which he knew many particulars.   I was obliged also, in my turn, to tell him stories of our Great King of Prussia, and his numerous armies, and also what sheep sold for in Prussia.   After we had thus been talking some time chiefly on political matters, he all at once asked me, if I could blow the French-horn? This he suppos'd I could do, only because I came from Germany, for, he said, he remembered, when he was a boy, a German had once stopped at this inn, with his parents, who blew the French-horn extremely well. _He therefore fancied this was a talent peculiar to the Germans.

I re

I removed this error, and we resumed our political topics, while his children, and servants, at some distance, listened with great respect to our conversation.

Thus I again spent a very agreeable evening, and when I had breakfasted in the morning, my bill was not more than it had been at Sutton. I at length reached the common before Derby, on Friday morning. The air was mild, and I seemed to feel myself uncommonly cheerful and happy. About noon the romantic part of the country began to open upon me. I came to a lofty eminence, where, all at once, I saw a boundless prospect of hills before me, behind which, fresh hills seemed always to arise, and to be infinite.

The ground now seemed undulatory, and to rise and fall like waves when at the summit of the rise, I seemed to be first raised aloft, and had an extensive view all around me, and the next moment, when I went down the hill, I lost it.

In the afternoon I saw Derby in the vale before me, and I was now an hundred and twenty six miles from London. Derby is but a small, and not very considerable, town. It was market day when I got there, and I

was

was obliged to pass through a crowd of people, but there was here no such odious curiosity, nor offensive staring, as at Burton.
Hereabouts too, I took notice, that I began
to be always civilly bowed to by the children
of the villages through which I passed.

From Derby, to the baths at Matlock,
which is one of the most romantic situations,
it was still fifteen miles. On my way thither,
I came to a long and extensive village, which
I believe was called *Duffield* They here at
least did not shew me into the kitchen, but
into the parlour, and I dined on cold victu-
als.

The prints and pictures, which I have generally seen at these inns, are, I think, almost always prints of the royal family, oftentimes in a group, where the king, as the father of the family, assembles his children
around him, or else I have found a Map of
London, and not seldom the portrait of the
king of Prussia, I have met with it several
times. You also sometimes see some of the
droll prints of Hogarth. The heat being
now very great, I several times in this village
heard the commiserating exclamation, of
" good God Almighty '" By which the peo-

ple

ple expreſſed their pity for me, as being a poor foot paſſenger.

At night I again ſtopped at an inn, on the road, about five miles from Matlock. I could eaſily have reached Matlock, but I wiſhed rather to reſerve the firſt view of the country, till the next day; than to get there when it was dark.

But I was not equally fortunate in this inn, as in the two former. The kitchen was full of farmers, among whom, I could not diſtinguiſh the landlord, whoſe health I ſhould otherwiſe immediately have drank. It is true I heard a country girl, who was alſo in the kitchen, as often as ſhe drank, ſay, "your health, gentlemen all!" But I do not know how it was, I forgot to drink any one's health, which I afterwards found, was taken much a-miſs. The landlord drank twice to my health, ſneeringly, as if to reprimand me for my incivility, and then began to join the reſt in ridiculing me; who almoſt pointed at me with their fingers. I was thus obliged for a time, to ſerve the farmers as a laughing ſtock, till at length one of them compaſſionately ſaid, "nay, nay, we muſt do him no "harm, for he is a ſtranger." The landlord,

lord, I suppose, to excuse himself, and as if he thought he had perhaps before gone too far, said, " ay, God forbid, we should hurt any " stranger," and ceased his ridicule : but when I was going to drink to his health, he slighted and refused my attention, and told me with a sneer, all I had to do, was to seat myself in the chimney corner, and not trouble myself about the rest of the world. The landlady seemed to pity me ; and so she led me into another room where I could be alone, saying . " what wicked people !"

I left this unfriendly roof early the next morning ; and now quickly proceeded to Matlock.

The extent of my journey I had now resolved should be the great Cavern near Castleton, in the high Peake of Derbyshire. It was about twenty miles beyond Matlock.

The country here had quite a different appearance, from that at Windsor and Richmond. Instead of green meadows and pleasant hills, I now saw barren mountains and lofty rocks, instead of fine living hedges, the fields, and pasture lands, here, were fenced with a wall of grey stone ; and of this very same stone, which is here every where to be found in plenty, all the houfes are built, in a very uniform and patriarchal manner, inafmuch as the rough ftones are almoft without any preparation, placed one upon another, and compofe four walls, fo that in cafe of neceffity, a man might here, without much trouble, build himfelf an houfe. At Derby the houfes feemed to be built of the fame ftone.

The fituation of Matlock itfelf furpaffed every idea I had formed of it. On the right were fome elegant houfes for the bathing company, and leffer cottages fufpended like bird's nefts in an high rock. To the left, deep in the bottom, there was a fine, bold river, which was almoft hid from the eye, by a majeftic arch, formed by high trees, which hung over it. A prodigious ftone wall extended itfelf above a mile along its border, and all along, there is a fingularly romantic and beautiful, fecret walk, fheltered and adorned by many beautiful fhrubs.

The fteep rock was covered at the top with green bufhes, and now and then a fheep, or a cow, feparated from the grazing flock, came o the edge of the precipice, and peeped over it.

I had

I had got in Milton's *Paradise Loſt*, which I
am reading regularly through, juſt to the
part where he deſcribes Paradiſe, when I arrived here, and the following paſſage, which
I read at the brink of the river, had a moſt
ſtriking and pleaſing effect on me.   The
landſcape here deſcribed, was as exactly ſimi-
lar to that I ſaw before me, as if the poet had
taken it from hence :

" ———————delicious Paradiſe,
" Now nearer, crowns with her encloſure green,
" As with a rural mound, the champain head
" Of a ſteep wilderneſs, whoſe hairy ſides
" With thicket overgrown, groteſque and wild,
" Acceſs denied."———————*Book* IV V 13⁷

From Matlock baths, you go over Matlock
bridge, to the little town of Matlock itſelf,
which, in reality, ſcarcely deſerves the name
of a village, as it conſiſts of but a few and mi-
ſerable houſes.   There is here, on account of
the baths, a number of horſes and carriages,
and a great thoroughfare.   From hence I
came through ſome villages to a ſmall town
of the name of Bakewell.   The whole country in this part is hilly and romantic   Often my
way led me by ſmall paſſes, over aſtoniſhing

K 6   emi-

eminences, where, in the deep below me, I
faw a few huts or cottages lying. The fen-
cing of the fields with grey ftone, gave to the
whole, a wild, and not very promifing, appearance,   The hills were in general not
wooded, but naked and barren; and you faw
the flocks at a diftance grazing on their fummit.

As I was coming through one of the villages, I heard a great farmer's boy eagerly
afk another, if he did not think I was a
Frenchman. It feemed as if he had been
waiting fometime, to fee the wonder; for,
he fpoke as though his wifh was now accomplifhed.

When I was paft Bakewell, a place far inferior to Derby, I came by the fide of a
broad river, to a fmall eminence, where a
fine cultivated field lay before me. This field,
all at once, made an indefcribable and very
pleafing impreffion on me, which, at firft, I
could not account for; till I recollected
having feen, in my childhood, near the village where I was educated, a fituation ftrikingly fimilar to that now before me, here in
England.

This

This field, as if it had been in Germany, was not enclosed with hedges, but every spot in it was uninterruptedly diversified, with all kinds of crops and growths of different green and yellowish colours, which gave the whole a most pleasing effect: but besides this large field, the general view of the country, and a thousand other little circumstances, which I cannot now particularly enumerate, served to bring back to my recollection the years of my youth.

Here I rested myself a-while; and when I was going on again, I thought on the place of my residence, on all my acquaintances, and not a little on you, my dearest friend, and imagined what you would think and say, if you were to see your friend thus wandering here all alone, totally unknown, and in a foreign land——And at that moment I first seriously felt the idea of distance; and the thought that I was now in England, so very far from all I loved, or who loved me, produced in me such sensations, as I have not often felt.

It was perhaps the same with you, my dearest friend, when on our journey to Hambro', we drove from Perlsbeg, to your birth-place, the village of Boberow; where, among the

far-

farmers, you again found your old playmates; one of whom was now become the bailiff of the place. On your afking them, whether they knew you, one and all of them anfwered fo heartily, " O, yes, yes,—why, you are " Mafter Frederick." The pedantic fchool-mafter, you will remember, was not fo frank. He expreffed himfelf in the ftiff town phrafe of, " he had not the honour of knowing you; " as during your refidence in that village, " when a child, he had not been *in loco*."

I now came through a little place of the name of Afhford, and wifhed to reach the fmall village of Wardlow, which was only three miles diftant, when two men came after me, at a diftance, whom I had already feen at Matlock, who called to me to wait for them. Thefe were the only foot paffengers, fince Mr Maud, who had offered to walk with me.

The one was a faddler, and wore a fhort brown jacket, and an apron, with a round hat. The other was very decently dreft, but a very filent man, whereas the faddler, was quite talkative.

I liftened with aftonifhment, when I heard him begin to fpeak of Homer, of Horace

and

and of Virgil, and ftill more when he quoted feveral paffages, by memory, from each of thefe authors, pronouncing the words, and laying his emphafis, with as much propriety as I could poffibly have expected, had he been educated at Cambridge, or at Oxford. He advifed me not to go to Wardlow, where I fhould find bad accommodations, but rather a few miles farther to *Tidefwell,* where he lived. This name is, by a fingular abbreviation, pronounced *Tidfel,* the fame as *Birmingham,* is called by the common people *Brummidgeham.*

We halted at a fmall ale houfe on the roadfide, where the faddler ftopped to drink, and talk, and from whence he was in no hafte to depart. He had the generofity and honour, however, to pay my fhare of the reckoning, becaufe, as he faid, he had brought me hither.

At no great diftance from the houfe, we came to a rifing ground, where my philofophical faddler made me obferve a profpect, which was perhaps the only one of the kind, in England. Below us was an hollow, not unlike an huge kettle, hollowed out of the furrounding mafs of earth, and at the bottom

of

of it, a little valley, where the green meadow
was divided, by a small rivulet that ran in fer-
pentine windings, its banks graced with the
moft inviting walks, behind a fmall winding,
there is juft feen an houfe where one of the
moft diftinguifhed inhabitants of this happy
vale, a great philofopher, lives retired, de-
dicating almoft all his time to his favourite
ftudies. He has tranfplanted a number of
foreign plants into his grounds. My guide
fell into almoft a poetic rapture, as he pointed
out to me the beauties of this vale, while our
third companion, who grew tired, became
impatient at our tedioufnefs.

We were now led by a fteep road to the
vale, through which we paffed, and then afcended again among the hills on the other
fide.

Not far from *Tidefwell,* our third companion left us, as he lived in a neighbouring
place. As we now at length faw *Tidefwell* lying before us in the vale, the faddler began to
give me an account of his family, adding, by
way of epifode, that he never quarrelled with
his wife; nor had ever once threatened her
with his fift, much lefs, ever lifted it againft
her. For his own fake, he faid, he never

called

called her names; nor gave her the lie.   I must here observe, that it is the greatest offence you can give any one in England, to say to him, *you lie*.   To be called a *liar*, is a still greater affront, and, *you are a damned liar*, is the very acme of vulgar abuse.

Just as in Germany, no one will bear the name of a *scoundrel*, or *knave*, or as in all quarrels, the bestowing such epithets on our adversary is the signal for fighting, so the term of *a liar* in England, is the most offensive, and is always resented by blows.   A man would never forgive himself, nor be forgiven, who could bear to be called *a liar*.

Our *Jacky* in London once looked at me with astonishment, on my happening to say to him in joke, *you are a liar*.   I assure you I had much to do, before I could pacify him.

If one may form a judgement of the character of a whole nation, from such little circumstances as this, I must say this rooted hatred of the word *liar*, appears to me to be no bad trait in the English

But to return to my travelling companion, who further told me, that he was obliged to earn his livelihood, at some distance from home, and that he was now returning for the

first

firſt time, for theſe two months, to his family.

He ſhewed me a row of trees near the
town, which he ſaid his father had planted,
and which therefore he never could look at
but with emotion, though he paſſed them
often, as he went backwards and forwards,
on his little journeys, to and from his birth
place. His father, he added, had once been
a rich man; but had expended all his foitune
to ſupport one ſon Unfortunately for himſelf,
as well as his family, his father had gone to
America, and left the reſt of his children
poor; notwithſtanding which, his memory
was ſtill dear to him, and he was always affected by the ſight of theſe trees.

Tideſwell conſiſts of two rows of low
houſes, built of rough grey ſtone. My guide,
immediately on our entrance into the place,
bade me take notice of the church, which
was very handſome, and notwithſtanding its
age, had ſtill ſome pretenſions to be conſi-
dered as an edifice built in the modern
taſte.

He now aſked me, whether he ſhould ſhew
me to a great inn, or to a cheap one. And as
I preferred the latter, he went with me himſelf

felf to a fmall public houfe, and very particularly recommended me to their care, as his fellow traveller, and a clever man, not without learning.

The people here alfo endeavoured to accommodate me moft magnificently, and for this purpofe gave me fome toafted cheefe, which was Chefhire cheefe, roafted and half melted at the fire. This, in England, it feems, is reckoned good eating, but unfortunately for me, I could not touch a bit of it. I therefore invited my landlord to partake of it, and he indeed, feemed to feaft on it. As I neither drank brandy, nor ale, he told me I lived far too fparingly for a foot traveller; he wondered how I had ftrength to walk fo well, and fo far.

I avail myfelf of this opportunity to obferve that the Englifh innkeepers are in general great ale drinkers, and for this reafon moft of them are grofs and corpulent: in particular they are plump and rofy in their faces. I once heard it faid of one of them, that the extravafated claret in his phiz, might well remind one, as Falftaff fays of Bardolph, of hell-fire.

The next morning my landlady did me the honour

honour to drink coffee with me, but helped
me, very sparingly, to milk and sugar. It
was Sunday, and I went with my landlord to
a barber, on whose shop was written " shaving
for a penny." There were a great many inhabitants assembled there, who took me for a
gentleman, on account, I suppose, of my hat;
which I had bought in London for a guinea,
and which they all admired. I considered
this as a proof, that pomp and finery had not
yet become general thus far from London.

You frequently find in England, at
many of the houses of the common people,
printed papers, with sundry apt and good
moral maxims and rules, fastened against the
room door, just as we find them in Germany.
On such wretched paper, some of the most
delightful and the finest sentiments may be
read, such as would do honour to any writer
of any country.

For instance, I read, among other things,
this golden rule, on such an ordinary printed
paper stuck against a room door, " Make no
comparisons." And if you consider how
many quarrels, and how much mischief arise
in the world, from odious comparisons of the
merits of one, with the merits of another,
the

the moſt delightful leſſons of morality are contained in the few words of the above mentioned rule.

A man, to whom I gave ſixpence, conducted me out of the town to the road leading
to Caſtleton, which was cloſe to a wall of ſtones,
confuſedly heaped one upon another, as I
have before deſcribed. The whole country
was hilly and rough, and the ground covered
with brown heath. Here, and there, ſome
ſheep were feeding.

I made a little digreſſion to an hill to the
left, where I had a proſpect, awfully beautiful, compoſed, almoſt entirely, of naked
rocks, far and near; among which, thoſe
that were entirely covered with black heath,
made a moſt tremendous appearance.

I was now an hundred and ſeventy miles
from London, when I aſcended one of the
higheſt hills, and all at once perceived a
beautiful vale below me, which was traverſed
by rivers and brooks, and encloſed on all
ſides by hills. In this vale lay Caſtleton, a
ſmall town, with low houſes, which takes its
name from an old Caſtle, whoſe ruins are ſtill
to be ſeen here.

A nar-

A narrow path, which wound itfelf down
the fide of the rock, led me through the vale
into the ftreet of Caftleton, where I foon found
an inn, and alfo foon dined. After dinner,
I made the beft of my way to the Cavern.

A little rivulet, which runs through the
middle of the town, led me to its entrance.

I ftood here a few moments, full of wonder,
and aftonifhment, at the amazing height, of
the fteep rock, before me, covered on each
fide with ivy and other fhrubs. At its fummit
are the decayed walls and towers of an ancient caftle which formerly ftood on this
rock, and at its foot, the monftrous aperture,
or mouth, to the entrance of the Cavern,
where it is pitch dark, when one looks down,
even at mid-day.

As I was ftanding here full of admiration, I
perceived, at the entrance of the cavern, a
man of a rude and rough appearance, who
afked me if I wifhed to fee the Peak; and
the echo ftrongly reverberated his coarfe
voice.

Anfwering, as I did, in the affirmative, he
next further afked me, if I fhould want to be
carried to the other fide of the ftream, telling

me, at the same time, what the sum would be, which I must pay for it.

This man had, along with his black stringy hair, and his dirty and tattered cloaths, such a singularly wild and infernal look, that he actually struck me as a real Charon; his voice and the questions he asked me, were not of a kind to remove this notion, so, that, far from its requiring any effort of imagination, I found it not easy to avoid believing, that, at length, I had actually reached Avernus, was about to cross Acheron, and to be ferried by Charon.

I had no sooner agreed to his demand, than he told me, all I had to do, was boldly to follow him; and thus we entered the Cavern.

To the left, in the entrance of the Cavern, lay the trunk of a tree, that had been cut down, on which several of the boys of the town were playing.

Our way seemed to be altogether on a descent, tho' not steep, so that the light, which came in at the mouth of the Cavern, near the entrance, gradually forsook us, and when we had gone forward a few steps farther, I was astonished by a sight, which of all others, I
here

here the leaft expected : I perceived to the right, in the hollow of the Cavern, a whole fubterranean village, where the inhabitants, on account of its being Sunday, were refting from their work; and with happy and cheaiful looks, were fitting at the doors of their huts, along with their children.

We had fcaicely paffed thefe fmall fubterranean houfes, when I perceived a number of large wheels, on which, on week days, thefe human moles, the inhabitants of the Cavein, make ropes.

I fancied I here faw the wheel of Ixion, and the inceffant labour of the Danaides.

The opening through which the light came, feemed, as we defcended, every moment to become lefs and lefs, and the darknefs at every ftep to encreafe, till at length only a few rays appeared, as if darting through a cievice, and juft tinging the fmall clouds of fmoke, which, at dufk, raifed themfelves to the mouth of the Cavern.

This gradual growth, or encreafe of darknefs, awakens in a contemplative mind, a foft melancholy. As you go down the gentle defcent of the Cavern, you can hardly help fancying, the moment is come, when, without

out pain or grief, the thread of life is about to be snapped, and that you are now going thus quietly to that land of peace, where trouble is no more.

At length the great Cavern in the rock closed itself, in the same manner as heaven and earth seem to join each other, when we came to a little door, where an old woman came out of one of the huts, and brought two candles, of which we each took one.

My guide now opened the door, which compleatly shut out the faint glimmering of light, which, till then, it was still possible to perceive, and led us to the inmost centre of this dreary temple of old Chaos, and Night, as if, till now, we had only been traversing the outer Courts. The rock was here so low, that we were obliged to stoop very much for some few steps, in order to get through, but how great was my astonishment when we had passed this narrow passage and again stood upright, at once to perceive, as well as the feeble light of our candles would permit, the amazing length, breadth, and height of the Cavern, compared to which, the monstrous opening through which we had already passed, was nothing.

L   After

here the leaft expected: I perceived to the right, in the hollow of the Cavern, a whole fubterranean village, where the inhabitants, on account of its being Sunday, were refting from their work, and with happy and chearful looks, were fitting at the doors of their huts, along with their children.

We had fcarcely paffed thefe fmall fubterranean houfes, when I perceived a number of large wheels, on which, on week days, thefe human moles, the inhabitants of the Cavern, make ropes.

I fancied I here faw the wheel of Ixion, and the inceffant labour of the Danaides.

The opening through which the light came, feemed, as we defcended, every moment to become lefs and lefs, and the darknefs at every ftep to encreafe, till at length only a few rays appeared, as if darting through a crevice, and juft tinging the fmall clouds of fmoke, which, at dufk, raifed themfelves to the mouth of the Cavern.

This gradual growth, or encreafe of darknefs, awakens in a contemplative mind, a foft melancholy. As you go down the gentle defcent of the Cavern, you can hardly help fancying, the moment is come, when, with-

out

out pain or grief, the thread of life is about to
be fnapped; and that you are now going thus
quietly to that land of peace, where trouble is
no more.

At length the great Cavern in the rock
clofed itfelf, in the fame manner as heaven and
earth feem to join each other, when we came
to a little door, where an old woman came
out of one of the huts, and brought two candles, of which we each took one.

My guide now opened the door, which
compleatly fhut out the faint glimmering of
light, which, till then, it was ftill poffible to
perceive, and led us to the inmoft centre of
this dreary temple of old Chaos, and Night,
as if, till now, we had only been travelfing
the outer Courts. The rock was here fo low,
that we were obliged to ftoop very much for
fome few fteps, in order to get through, but
how great was my aftonifhment when we had
paffed this narrow paffage and again ftood upright, at once to perceive, as well as the feeble light of our candles would permit, the
amazing length, breadth, and height of the
Cavern, compared to which, the monftrous
opening through which we had already paffed,
was nothing.

After we had wandered here more than an hour, as beneath a dark and dusky sky, on a level sandy soil, the rock gradually lowered itself, and we suddenly found ourselves on the edge of a broad river, which, from the glimmering of our candles amid the total darkness, suggested sundry interesting reflections. To the side of this river, a small boat was moor'd, with some straw in its bottom. Into this boat, my guide desired me to step, and lay myself down in it quite flat, because, as he said, towards the middle of the river, the rock would almost touch the water.

When I had laid myself down, as directed, he himself jumped into the water, and drew the boat after him.

All around us, was one still, solemn, and deadly silence, and as the boat advanced, the rock seemed to stoop, and come nearer and nearer to us, till at length it nearly touched my face, and as I lay I could hardly hold the candle upright. I seemed to myself to be in a coffin, rather than in a boat, as I had no room to stir hand or foot, till we had passed this frightful strait, and the rock rose again on the other side; where my guide once more handed me a shore.

The

The Cavern was now become, all at once broad and high, and then, suddenly, it was again low and narrow.

I observed on both sides, as we passed along, a prodigious number of great, and small petrified plants, and animals, which however we could not examine, unless we had been disposed to spend some days in the Cavern.

And thus we arrived at the opposite side, at the second river or stream, which however was not so broad as the first, as one may see across it, to the other side. across this stream my guide carried me on his shoulders, because there was here no boat to carry us over.

From thence we only went a few steps farther, when we came to a very small piece of water, which extended itself length-ways; and led us to the end of the Cavern.

The path, along the edge of this water, was wet and slippery, and sometimes so very narrow, that one can hardly set one foot before the other.

Notwithstanding, I wandered with pleasure on this subterranean shore, and was regaling myself with the interesting contemplation of all these various wonderful objects, in this land of darkness, and shadow of Death, when,

L 2

all

all at once fomething like mufic at a diftance, founded in mine ears.

I inftantly ftopped, full of aftonifhment; and eagerly afked my guide, what this might mean? He anfwered, only, have patience, and you fhall foon fee.

But as we advanced, the founds of harmony feemed to die away; the noife became weaker and weaker, and at length, it feemed to fink into a gentle hiffing, or hum, like diftant drops of falling rain.

And how great was my amazement, when ere long I actually faw and felt a violent fhower of rain falling from the rock, as from a thick cloud, whofe drops, which now fell on our candles, had caufed that fame melancholy found, which I had heard at a diftance.

This was what is here called a *mizzling rain*; which fell from the ceiling or roof of the Cavern, through the veins of the rock.

We did not dare to approach too near with our candles, as they might eafily have been extinguifhed by the falling drops; and fo we perhaps have been forced to feek our way back in vain.

We continued our march therefore along the fide of the water, and often faw on the

fides

fides large apertures in the rock; which feemed to be new or fubordinate Caverns, all which we paffed without looking into. At length my guide prepared me for one of the fineft fights we had yet feen, which we fhould now foon behold.

- And we had hardly gone on a few paces, when we entered what might eafily be taken for a Majeftic Temple, with lofty arches, fupported by beautiful pillars; formed by the plaftic hand of fome ingenious artift.

This fubterranean Temple, in the ftructure of which no human hand had borne a part, appeared to me at that moment to furpafs all the moft ftupendous buildings in the world, in point of regularity, magnificence and beauty.

Full of admiration and reverence, here even in the inmoft receffes of Nature, I faw the Majefty of the Creator difplayed, and before I quitted this Temple, here in this folemn filence, and holy gloom, I thought it would be a becoming act of true religion to adore, as I cordially did, the God of Nature.

We now drew near the end of our journey. Our faithful companion, the water, guided us

through

through the remainder of the Cavern, where the rock is arched for the laft time, and then finks till it touches the water which here forms a femi-circle, and thus the Cavern clofes, fo that no mortal can go one ftep farther.

My guide here again jumped into the water, fwam a little way under the rock; and then came back, quite wet, to fhew me, that it was impoffible to go any further, unlefs this rock could be blown up with powder, and a fecond Cavern opened I now thought, all we had to do, was to return the neareft way; but there were new difficulties ftill to encounter, and new fcenes to behold, ftill more beautiful than any I had yet feen.

My guide now turned and went back towards the left, where I followed him through a large opening in the rock.

And here he firft afked me if I could determine to creep a confiderable diftance through the rock, where it nearly touched the ground? Having confented to do fo, he told me I had only to follow him, warning me, at the fame time, to take great care of my candle.

Thus we crept on our hands and feet, on the wet and muddy ground, through the opening in the rock, which was often fcarcely

large

large enough for us to get through with our bodies.

When, at length, we had got through this troublesome passage, I saw, in the Cavern, a steep hill, which was so high, that it seemed to lose itself as in a cloud, in the summit of the rock.

This hill was so wet and slippery, that, as soon as I attempted to ascend, I fell down My guide however took hold of my hand, and told me, I had only resolutely, to follow him.

We now ascended such an amazing height, and there were such precipices on each side, that it makes me giddy even now, when I think of it.

When we at length had gained the summit, where the hill seemed to lose itself in the rock, my guide placed me where I could stand firm , and told me to stay there quietly. In the mean time he himself went down the hill with his candle, and left me alone

I lost sight of him for some moments but at length I perceived not him indeed, but his candle, quite in the bottom, from whence it seemed to shine like a bright and twinkling star.

After I had enjoyed this indescribably beau-

L 4

tiful fight for fometime, my guide came back, and carried me fafely, down the hill again, on his fhoulders. And as I now ftood below, he went up and let his candle fhine again through an opening of the rock, while I covered mine with my hand, and it was now as if on a dark night a bright Star fhone down upon me: a fight which, in point of beauty, far furpaffed all that I had ever feen.

Our journey was now ended and we returned not without trouble and difficulty, through the narrow paffage. We again entered the Temple we had a fhort time before left, again heard the pattering of the rain, which founded as rain, when we were near it, but which, at a diftance, feemed a fonorous, dull, and melancholy hum: and now again we returned acrofs the quiet ftreams through the capacious entrance of the Cavern, to the little door, where we had before taken our leave of day-light: which after fo long a darknefs, we now again hailed with joy.

Before my guide opened the door he told me, I fhould now have a view of a fight that would furpafs all the foregoing. I found that he was in the right; for when he had only half

opened

opened the door, it really feemed as if I was looking into Elyfium.

The day feemed to be gradually breaking, and night and darknefs to have vanifhed. At a diftance, you again juft faw the fmoke of the cottages, and then the cottages themfelves, and, as we afcended, we faw the boys ftill playing around the hewn trunk, till at length the reddifh purple ftripes, in the fky, faintly appeared through the mouth of the hole yet, juft as we came out, the fun was fetting in the Weft.

Thus had I fpent nearly the whole afternoon, till it was quite evening, in the Cavern; and when I looked at myfelf, I was, as to my drefs, not much unlike my Guide: my fhoes fcarcely hung to my feet, they were fo foft and fo torn by walking fo long on the damp fand, and the hard pointed ftones.

I paid no more than half-a-crown for feeing all that I had feen, with a trifle to my Guide: for, it feems, he does not get the half-crown, but is obliged to account for it to his mafter, who lives very comfortably on the revenue he derives from this Cavern, and is able to keep a man to fhew it to ftrangers.

L 5

When

When I came home I fent for a fhoe-maker.
There was one who lived juft oppofite, and
he immediately came to examine my fhoes.
He told me he could not fufficiently wonder at
the badnefs of the work, for they were fhoes
I had brought from Germany. Notwithftanding this, he undertook, as he had no new ones
ready, to mend them for me as well as he
could.   This led me to make a very agreeable acquaintance with this fhoe-maker: for,
when I expreffed to him my admiration of the
Cave in, it pleafed him greatly that in fo infignificant a place as Caftleton, there fhould
be any thing which could infpire people with
aftonifhment, who came from fuch diftant
countries, and thereupon offered to take a
walk with me, to fhew me, at no great diftance, the famous mountain called *Mam-Tor*,
which is reckoned among the things of moft
note in Derbyfhire.

This mountain, is covered with verdure on
its fummit, and fides, but at the end it is a
fteep precipice.   The middle part does not,
like other mountains, confift of rock, but of
a loofe earth, which gives way, and either
rolls from the top of the precipice in little
pieces, or tears itfelf loofe in large maffes, and
falls

falls with a thundering crash, thus forming an hill on its side which is continually encreasing.

From these circumstances probably is derived the name of *Mam-Tor*, which literally signifies *Mother Hill*, for *Tor*, is either an abbreviation of, or the old word for, *Tower*; and means not only a lofty building, but any eminence Mam, is a familiar term, that obtains, in all languages, for Mother, and this Mountain, like a Mother, produces several other small hills.

The inhabitants here have a superstitious notion, that this mountain, notwithstanding its daily loss, never decreases, but always keeps its own, and remains the same.

My companion told me a shocking history of an inhabitant of Castleton, who laid a wager, that he would ascend this steep precipice.

As the lower part is not quite so steep, but rather slanting upwards, he could get good hold in this soft loose earth, and clambered up, without looking round. At length he had gained more than half the ascent, and was just at the part, where it projects and overlooks its basis, from this astonishing height the unfortunate man cast down his eyes, whilst

L 6

the

the threatning point of the rock hung over him, with tottering maſſes of earth.

He trembled all over, and was juſt going to relinquiſh his hold, not daring to move backwards or forwards: in this manner he hung for ſome time between heaven and earth, ſurrounded by deſpair. However, his ſinews would bear it no longer; and therefore, in an effort of deſpair, he once more collected all his ſtrength, and got hold of, firſt, one looſe ſtone, and then another; all of which would have failed him, had he not immediately caught hold of another. By theſe means, however, at length, to his own, as well as to the aſtoniſhment of all the ſpectators, he avoided almoſt inſtant and certain death, ſafely gained the ſummit of the hill, and won his wager

I trembled as I heard this relation; ſeeing the mountain and the precipice in queſtion ſo near to me, I could not help figuring to myſelf the man clambering up it.

Not far from hence is *Elden Hole*, a cavity, or pit, or hole in the earth, of ſuch a monſtrous depth, that if you throw in a pebble ſtone, and lay your ear to the hedge of the hole, you hear it falling for a long time.

As

As foon as it comes to the bottom it emits a found juft as if fome one were uttering a loud figh. The firft noife it makes, on its being firft parted with, affects the ear like a fubterranean thunder. This rumbling, or thundering noife, continues for fome time, and then decreafes, as the ftone falls againft firft one hard rock and then another, at a greater and a greater depth ; and at length when it has for fometime been falling, the noife ftops with a kind of whizzing, or a hiffing, murmur. The people have alfo a world of fuperftitious ftories relating to this place , one of which is, that fome perfon once threw into it a goofe, which appeared again, at two miles diftance, in the great cavern I have already mentioned, quite ftripped of its feathers ·——But I will not ftuff my letters with many of thefe fabulous hiftories.

They reckon that they have in Derbyfhire feven wonders of nature; of which, this *Elden Hole*, the hill of *Man-Tor*, and the great cavern, I have been at, are the principal. This cavern goes commonly by a name that is fhockingly vulgar . in Englifh it is called *The Devil's Arfe o' Peak*.

The remaining four wonders are *Pool's Hole*,

Hole, which has some resemblance to this that I have seen, as I am told, for I did not see it, next, *St. Ann's Well,* where there are two springs, which rise close to each other; the one of which is boiling-hot, the other as cold as ice, the next is, *Tide's-well,* not far from the town of that name, through which I passed. It is a spring, or well, which in general flows or runs under ground, imperceptibly, and then all at once rushes forth with a mighty rumbling or subterranean noise, which is said to have something musical in it, and overflows its banks. Lastly, *Chatsworth,* a palace, or seat, belonging to the Dukes of Devonshire, at the foot of a mountain, whose summit is covered with eternal snow, and therefore always gives one the idea of winter, at the same time that the most delightful spring blooms at its foot. I can give you no further description of these latter wonders, as I only know them by the account given me by others. They were the subjects with which my guide, the shoe-maker, entertained me during our walk.

While this man was shewing me every thing within his knowledge, that he thought most interesting, he often expressed his admiration

on

on thinking how much of the world I had already feen, and the idea excited in him fo lively a defire to travel, that I had much to do to reafon him out of it. He could not help talking of it the whole evening, and again and again protefted, that, had he not got a wife and a child, he would fet off in the morning, at day-break, along with me, for here in Caftleton there is but little to be earned by the hardeft labour, or even genius; provifions are not cheap; and in fhort, there is no fcope for exertion.—This honeft man was not yet thirty.

As we returned, he wifhed yet to fhew me the lead mines, but it was too late. Yet, late as it was, he mended my fhoes the fame evening, and I muft do him the juftice to add, in a very mafterly manner.

But I am forry to tell you, I have brought a cough from the cavern, that does not at all pleafe me, indeed it occafions me no little pain, which makes me fuppofe that one muft needs breathe a very unwholefome damp air in this cavern. But then, were that the cafe, I do not comprehend how my friend *Charon* fhould have held it out fo long, and fo well, as he has.

This

This morning I was up very early in order to view the ruins, and to climb an high hill, along-side of them. The ruins, are directly over the mouth of the hole on the hill, which extends itself some distance over the cavern, beyond the ruins, and always widens, though here in front it is so narrow, that the building takes up the whole.

From the ruins all around, there is nothing but steep rock, so that there is no access to it, but from the town, where a crooked path from the foot of the hill is hewn in the rock, but it is also prodigiously steep.

The spot on which the ruins stand, is now all overgrown with nettles and thistles. Formerly, it is said, there was a bridge from this mountain, to the opposite one, of which one may yet discover some traces, as in the vale, which divides the two rocks, we still find the remains of some of the arches on which the bridge rested This vale which lies at the back of the ruins, and probably over the cavern, is called the *Cave's Way*, and is one of the greatest thoroughfares to the town. In the part, at which, at some distance, it begins to descend between these two mountains, its descent is so gentle that one is not at

all

all tired in going down it. But if you fhould happen to mifs the way between the two rocks, and continue on the heights, you are in great danger of falling from the rock, which every moment becomes fteeper and fteeper.

The mountain, on which the ruins ftand, is every where rocky. The one on the left of it, which is feparated by the vale, is perfectly ver dant and fertile, and, on its fummit, the pafture lands are divided by ftones, piled up in the form of a wall. This green mountain is at leaft three times as high as that on which the ruins ftand.

I began to clamber up the green mountain, which is alfo pretty fteep, and when I had got more than half way up without having once looked back, I was nearly in the fame fituation as the adventurer who clambered up *Mam-Tor* hill; for when I looked round, I found my eye had not been trained to view, unmoved, fo prodigious an height; Caftleton, with the furrounding country, lay below me, like a map; the roofs of the houfes feemed almoft clofe to the ground, and the mountain, with the ruins itfelf, feemed to be lying at my feet.

I grew giddy at the profpect, and it re-
quired

quired all my reafon to convince me that I was in no danger, and that, at all events, I could only fcramble down the green turf, in the fame manner as I had got up. At length I feemed to grow accuftomed to this view, till it really gave me pleafure, and I now climbed quite to the fummit, and walked over the meadows, and at length reached the way, which gradually defcends between the two mountains.

At the top of the green mountain I met with fome neat country girls, who were milking their cows, and coming this fame way with their milk-pails on their heads.

This little rural party formed a beautiful group, when fome of them with their milk-pails took fhelter, as it began to rain, under a part of the rock, beneath which they fat down on natural ftone benches, and there, with paftoral innocence and glee, talked and laughed till the fhower was over.

My way led me into the town, from whence I now write, and which I intend leaving in order to begin my journey back to London, but I think I fhall not now purfue quite the fame road.

NORTHAMPTON.

NORTHAMPTON.

WHEN I took leave of the honeſt ſhoe-maker, in Caſtleton, who would have rejoiced to have accompanied me, I reſolved to return, not by *Tide's-well*, but by *Wardlow*, which is nearer.

I there found but one ſingle inn, and in it only a landlady, who told me that her huſband was at work in the lead-mines; and that the cavern at Caſtleton, and all that I had yet ſeen, was nothing to be compared to theſe lead-mines. Her huſband, ſhe ſaid, would be happy to ſhew them to me.

When I came to offer to pay her for my dinner, ſhe made ſome difficulty about it; becauſe, as I had neither drank ale, or brandy, by the ſelling of which ſhe chiefly made her livelihood, ſhe ſaid ſhe could not well make out my bill. On this I called for a mug of ale (which I did not drink) in order to enable me the better to ſettle her reckoning.

At this ſame inn I ſaw my inn-keeper of Tideſwell, who, however, had not, like me, come on foot, but prancing proudly on horſe-back.

As

As I proceeded, and saw the hills rise before me, which were still fresh in my memory, having so recently become acquainted with them, in my journey thither, I was just reading the passage, in Milton, relative to the creation, in which the Angel describes to Adam how the waters subsided, and

" Immediately the mountains huge appear
" Emergent, and their broad bare backs upheave
" Into the clouds, their tops ascend the sky."

BOOK vii. l. 285.

It seemed to me, while reading this passage, as if every thing around me were in the act of creating, and the mountains themselves appeared to emerge or rise; so animated was the scene.

I had felt something, not very unlike this, on my journey hither; as I was sitting opposite to an hill, whose top was covered with trees, and was reading in Milton the sublime description of the combat of the Angels, where the fallen Angels are made, with but little regard to chronology, to attack their antagonists with artillery and cannon, as if it had been a battle on earth, of the present age. The better Angels, however, defend them-

felves

felves againft their *antagonifts*, by each feizing on fome hill, by the tufts on its fummit, tearing them up by the root, and thus bearing them in their hands, to fling them at their enemy.

" ————————they ran, they flew,
" From their foundation loos'ning to and fro,
" They pluck'd the feated hills with all their load,
" Rocks, waters, woods, and by the fhaggy tops
" Uplifting bore them in their hands————."

Book vi. l. 642.

I feemed to fancy to myfelf, that I actually faw an Angel there ftanding and plucking up an hill before me and fhaking it in the air.

When I came to the laft village, before I got to Matlock, as it was now evening and dark, I determined to fpend the night there; and enquired for an inn, which, I was told, was at the end of the village. And fo on I walked, and kept walking till near midnight, before I found this fame inn. The place feemed to have no end. On my journey to Caftleton, I muft either not have paffed through this village or not have noticed its length. Much tired, and not a little indif-pofed, I, at length, arrived at the inn, where I fat myfelf down by the fire in the kitchen,

and

and afked for fomething to eat.   As they told me, I could not have a bed here, I replied I abfolutely would not be driven away, for that if nothing better could be had, I would fit all night by the fire.   This I actually prepared to do, and laid my head on the table in order to fleep.

When the people, in the kitchen, thought that I was afleep, I heard them talking about me, and guefling who, or what I might be. One woman alone feemed to take my part, and faid, " I dare fay, he is a well-bred gentleman;" another fcouted that notion merely becaufe, as fhe faid, I had come on foot, and " depend on it," faid fhe, " he is fome poor travelling " creature !"   My ears yet ring with the contemptuous tone with which fhe uttered, " Poor travelling creature !" It feems to express, all the wretchednefs of one, who neither has houfe, nor home, a vagabond, and outcaft of fociety.

At laft, when thefe unfeeling people faw that I was determined, at all events, to flay there all night, they gave me a bed, but not till I had long given up all hopes of getting one. And in the morning, when they afked me a fhilling for it, I gave them half-a-crown,

adding,

adding, with something of an air, that I would have no change.   This I did, though, perhaps, foolishly, to shew them, that I was not quite *a poor creature*.   And now they took leave of me with great civility, and many excuses, and I now continued my journey much at my ease.

When I had passed Matlock, I did not go again towards Derby, but took the road to the left towards Nottingham.   Here the hills gradually disappeared, and my journey now lay through meadow grounds, and cultivated fields.

I must here inform you, that the word *Peake*, or *Pike*, in old English, signifies a point or summit, the *Peak* of Derbyshire, therefore means that part of the country, which is hilly, or where the mountains are highest.

Towards noon I again came to an eminence, where I found but one single solitary inn, which had a singular inscription on its sign. It was in rhime, and I remember only that it ended with these words, " Refresh and then go " on." ' Entertainment for man and horse." This I have seen on several signs, but the most common, at all the lesser ale-houses, is
" A.

" A. B. C. or D. Dealer in foreign fpirituous
" liquors."

I dined here on cold meat and fallad. This,
or elfe *eggs and fallad*, was my ufual fupper,
and my dinner too, at the inns at which I
ftopped. It was but feldom that I had the
good fortune to get any thing hot. The fallad, for which they brought me all the ingre-
dients, I was always obliged to drefs myfelf.
This, I believe, is always done in England.

The road was now tolerably pleafant, but
the country feemed here to be uniform and
unvaried even to dullnefs. However, it was
a very fine evening, and as I paffed through a
village, juft before fun-fet, feveral people,
who met me accofted me with a phrafe, which
at firft, I thought odd, but which I now
think civil, if not polite. As if I could poffibly want information on fuch a point, as they
paffed me, they all very courteoufly told me
'twas a fine evening, or *a pleafant night*.

I have alfo often met people who, as they
paffed me, obligingly and kindly afked: *how
do you do?* To which unexpected queftion
from total ftrangers, I have now learned to
anfwer—*pretty well I thank you, how do you do?*
—This manner of addrefs muft needs appear
very

very fingular to a foreigner, who is all at once afked by a perfon, whom he has never feen before, how he does?

After I had paffed through this village, I came to a green field, at the fide of which I met with an ale-houfe. The miftrefs was fitting at the window, I afked her, if I could ftay the night there, fhe faid no! and fhut the window in my face.

This unmannerlinefs recalled to my recollection, the many receptions of this kind to which I had now fo often been expofed; and I could not forbear uttering aloud my indignation at the inhofpitality of the Englifh; this harfh fentiment I foon corrected, however, as I walked on, by recollecting, and placing in the oppofite fcale, the unbounded and unequalled generofity of this nation, and alfo the many acts of real and fubftantial kindnefs, which I had myfelf experienced in it.

I at laft came to another inn, where there was written on the fign. " The Navigation " Inn," becaufe it is the *depôt*, or ftorehoufe, of the colliers of the Trent.

A rougher or ruder kind of people I never faw than thefe colliers, whom I here met af-

M   fembled

sembled in the kitchen, and in whose company I was obliged to spend the evening.

Their language, their dress, their manners, were, all of them, singularly vulgar and disagreeable; and their expressions still more so: For, they hardly spoke a word, without adding, *a G— d—— me* to it, and thus cursing, quarrelling, drinking, singing, and fighting, they seemed to be pleased, and to enjoy the evening. I must do them the justice to add, that none of them, however, at all molested me, or did me any harm. On the contrary, every one again and again drank my health, and I took care not to forget to drink theirs in return. The treatment of my host at Matlock was still fresh in my memory; and so, as often as I drank, I never omitted saying "Your healths, gentlemen all!"

When two Englishmen quarrel, the fray is carried on, and decided, rather by actions than by words, though loud and boisterous, they do not say much, and frequently repeat the same thing over and over again, always clinching it with an additional *G— d——you!* Their anger seems to overpower their utterance, and can find vent only by coming to blows.

The

The landlady, who fat in the kitchen along with all this goodly company, was neverthelefs well dreffed, and a remarkably well-looking woman. As foon as I had fupped, I haftened to bed, but could not fleep; my quondam companions, the colliers, made fuch a noife the whole night through.——In the morning, when I got up, there was not one to be feen, nor heard.

I was now only a few miles from Nottingham, where I arrived towards noon.

This, of all the towns I have yet feen, except London, feemed to me to be one of the beft, and is undoubtedly the cleaneft. Every thing here wore a modern appearance, and a large place in the centre, fcarcely yielded to a London fquare, in point of beauty.

From the town a charming foot-path leads you acrofs the meadows to the high-road, where there is a bridge over the Trent. Not far from this bridge was an inn, where I dined, though I could get nothing but bread and butter, of which I defired to have a toaft made.

Nottingham lies high, and made a beautiful appearance at a diftance, with its neat high houfes, red-roofs and its lofty fteeples.   I

M 2

have

have not feen fo fine a profpect in any other town in England.

I now came through feveral villages, as Ruddington, Bradmore and Bunny to Caftol, where I ftayed all night.

This whole afternoon I heard the ringing of bells in many of the villages. Probably, it is fome holiday which they thus celebrate. It was cloudy weather, and I felt myfelf not at all well, and in thefe circumftances this ringing difcompofed me ftill more, and made me at length quite low fpirited and melancholy.

At Caftol there were three inns clofe to each other, in which, to judge only from the outfide of the houfes, little but poverty was to be expected. In the one at which I at length ftopped there was only a landlady, a fick butcher, and a fick carter, - both of whom had come there to ftay the night. This affemblage of fick perfons gave me the idea of an hofpital, and depreffed me ftill more. I felt fome degree of fever, was very reftlefs all night, and fo I kept my bed very late the next morning, 'till the woman of the houfe came and aroufed me, by faying fhe had been uneafy on my account. And now I formed the refolution to go to Leicefter in the poft coach.

I was

I was now only four miles from Loughborough, a small, and I think, not a very handsome town, where I arrived late at noon, and dined at the last inn on the road that leads to Leicester. Here again, far beyond expectation, the people treated me like a gentleman, and let me dine in the parlour.

From Loughborough to Leicester, was only ten miles, but the road was sandy and very unpleasant walking.

I came through a village called *Mountforrel*, which perhaps takes its name from a little hill at the end of it. As for the rest, it was all one large plain, all the way to Leicester.

Towards evening I came to a pleasant meadow just before I got to Leicester, through which a foot-path led me to the town, which made a good appearance as I viewed it lengthways, and indeed much larger than it really is.

I went up a long street before I got to the house from which the post-coaches set out, and which is also an inn. I here learnt that the stage was to set out that evening for London, but that the inside was already full, some places were however still left on the outside.

Being

Being obliged to beftir myfelf to get back to London, as the time drew near, when the Hambro' captain, with whom I intend to return, had fixed his departure, I determined to take a place as far as Northampton on the outfide.

But this ride from Leicefter to Northampton, I fhall remember as long as I live.

The coach drove from the yard through a part of the houfe. The infide paffengers got in, in the yard; but we on the outfide were obliged to clamber up in the public ftreet, becaufe we fhould have had no room for our heads to pafs under the gateway.

My companions on the top of the coach, were a farmer, a young man very decently dreffed, and a black-a-moor.

The getting up alone was at the rifk of one's life, and when I was up, I was obliged to fit juft at the corner of the coach, with nothing to hold by, but a fort of little handle, faftened on the fide. I fat neareft the wheel, and the moment that we fet off, I fancied that I faw certain death await me. All I could do, was to take ftill fafter hold of the handle, and to be more and more careful to preferve my balance.

The

The machine now rolled along with prodigious rapidity, over the ſtones through the
town, and every moment we ſeemed to fly
into the air; ſo that it was almoſt a miracle,
that we ſtill ſtuck to the coach, and did not
fall.   We ſeemed to be thus on the wing,
and to fly, as often as we paſſed through a
village, or went down an hill.

At laſt the being continually in fear of my
life, became inſupportable, and as we were
going up a hill, and conſequently proceed-
ing rather ſlower than uſual, I crept from
the top of the coach, and got ſnug into the
baſket.

" O, ſir, ſir, you will be ſhaken to death !"
ſaid the black; but I flattered myſelf, he ex-
aggerated the unpleaſantneſs of my poſt.

As long as we went up hill, it was eaſy and
pleaſant.   And, having had little or no ſleep
the night before, I was almoſt aſleep among
the trunks and the packages, but how was
the caſe altered when we came to go down
hill, then all the trunks and parcels began, as
it were, to dance around me, and every thing
in the baſket ſeemed to be alive, and I every
moment received from them ſuch violent
blows, that I thought my laſt hour was come. I

M 4   now

now found that what the black had told me, was no exaggeration, but all my complaints were uſeleſs.   I was obliged to ſuffer this torture nearly an hour, till we came to another hill again, when quite ſhaken to pieces and ſadly bruiſed, I again crept to the top of the coach, and took poſſeſſion of my former ſeat. " Ah, did not I tell you, that you would be " ſhaken to death?" ſaid the black, as I was getting up, but I made him no reply. Indeed I was aſhamed; and I now write this as a warning to all ſtrangers to ſtage-coaches who may happen to take it into their heads, without being uſed to it, to take a place on the outſide of an Engliſh poſt-coach, and ſtill more, a place in the baſket.

About midnight we arrived at Harborough, where I could only reſt myſelf a moment, before we were again called to ſet off, full drive, through a number of villages, ſo that a few hours before day-break we had reached Northampton, which is, however, thirty three miles from Leiceſter.

From Harborough to Leiceſter, I had a moſt dreadful journey, it rained inceſſantly; and as before we had been covered with duſt, we now were ſoaked with rain.   My neighbour,

bour, the young man, who fat next me in the middle, that my inconveniences might be compleat, every now and then fell afleep; and, as when afleep, he perpetually bolted and rolled againft me, with the whole weight of his body, more than once he was very near pufhing me entirely off my feat

We at laft reached Northampton, where I immediately went to bed, and have flept almoft till noon. To-morrow morning I intend to continue my journey to London in fome other ftage-coach.

LONDON, 14TH JULY, 1782.

THE journey from Northampton to London
I can again hardly call a journey; but rather
a perpetual motion, or removal, from one
place to another, in a close box . during your
conveyance you may, perhaps, if you are in
luck, converse with two or three people shut
up along with you.

But I was not so fortunate , for my three
travelling companions, were all farmers, who
slept so soundly, that even the hearty knocks
of the head with which they often saluted
each other, did not awake them.

Their faces, bloated and discoloured by
their copious use of ale and brandy, looked,
as they lay before me, like so many lumps of
dead flesh.   When now and then they woke,
sheep, in which they all dealt, was the first
and last topic of their conversation One of the
three, however, differed not a little from the
other two: his face was sallow and thin, his
eyes quite sunk and hollow, his long lank
fingers hung quite loose, and as if detached
from his hands. He was, in short, the picture
of avarice and misanthrophy. The former

he

he certainly was; for at every stage he refused
to give the coachman the accustomed per-
quisite, which every body else paid, and
every farthing he was forced to part with,
forced a G—d d—n, from his heart. As he
sat in the coach, he seemed anxious to shun
the light, and so shut up every window that
he could come at, except, when now and then
I opened them to take a slight view of the
charms of the country through which we
seemed to be flying, rather than driving.

Our road lay through Newport-Pagnel,
Dunstable, St. Albans, Barnet to Islington, or
rather to London itself. But these names are
all I know of the different places

At Dunstable, if I do not mistake, we
breakfasted, and here, as is usual, every
thing was paid for in common by all the passengers, as I did not know this, I ordered
coffee separately; however, when it came,
the three farmers also drank of it, and gave
me some of their tea.

They asked me, what part of the world I
came from, whereas we in Germany generally
inquire, what countryman a person is.

When we had breakfasted, and were again
seated in the coach, all the farmers, the lean

M 6

one excepted, feemed quite alive again, and now began a converfation on religion and on politics.

One of them brought the hiftory of Samfon on the carpet, which the clergyman of his parifh, he faid, had lately explained, I dare fay, very fatisfactorily; though this honeft farmer ftill had a great many doubts about the great gate which Samfon carried away, and about the foxes with the fire-brands between their tails In other refpects, however, the man feemed not to be either uninformed or fceptical.

They now proceeded to relate to each other various ftories chiefly out of the Bible; not merely as important facts, but as interefting narratives, which they would have told and liftened to with equal fatisfaction, had they met them anywhere elfe. One of them had only heard thefe ftories from his minifter in the church, not being able to read them himfelf.

The one that fat next to him now began to talk about the Jews of the Old Teftament, and affured us that the prefent race were all defcended from thofe old ones. " Aye, and " they are all damned to all eternity !"—faid

his

his companion, as coolly and as confidently as if at that moment he had feen them burning in the bottomlefs pit.

We now frequently took up frefh paffengers, who only rode a fhort diftance with us, and then got out again. Among others, was a woman from London, whofe bufinefs was, the making of brandy. She entertained us with a very circumftantial narrative of all the fhocking fcenes, during the late riot in that city. What particularly ftruck me was her faying, that fhe faw a man, oppofite to her houfe, who was fo furious, that he ftood on the wall of a houfe that was already half burnt down, and there, like a dæmon, with his own hands pulled down and toffed about the bricks which the fire had fpared, till at length he was fhot, and fell back among the flames.

At length we arrived at London without any accident, in a hard rain, about one o'clock. I had been obliged to pay fixteen fhillings before-hand at Northampton, for the fixty miles to London. This the coachman feemed not to know for certain, and therefore afked me more earneftly, if I was fure I had paid. I affured him I had, and he took my word.

I looked

I looked like a crazy creature, when I arrived in London, notwithstanding which, Mr. Pointer, with whom I left my trunk, received me in the most friendly manner, and desired me during dinner to relate to him my adventures.

The same evening I called on Mr. Leonhardi, who, as I did not wish to hire a lodging for the few days I might be obliged to wait for a fair wind, got me into the Freemason's-tavern. And here I have been waiting these eight days, and the wind still continues contrary for Hambro'; though I do now most heartily wish for a fair wind, as I can no longer make any improvement, by my stay, since I must keep myself in constant readiness to embark whenever the wind changes, and therefore I dare go no great distance.

Every body here is now full of the Marquis of Rockingham's death, and the change of the ministry in consequence of it. They are much displeased that Fox has given up his seat; and yet it is singular, they still are much concerned, and interest themselves for him, as if whatever interested him, were the interest of the nation.

On

On Tuefday there was an highly impoitant debate in Parliament. Fox was called on to affign the true reafons of his iefignation before the nation. At eleven o'clock the gallery was fo full, that nobody could get a place; and the debates only begin at three, and lafted this evening till ten.

About four, Fox came. Every one was full of expectation. He fpoke at firft with gieat vehemence, but it was obferved that he gradually became moie and more modeiate, and when at length he had vindicated the ftep he had taken, and fhewed it to be, in every point of view, juft, wife, and honouiable,— he added, with great force and pathos, "and now I ftand here once moie, as poor as "ever I was." It was impoffible to hear fuch a fpeech and fuch declarations unmoved.

General Conway then gave his reafons, why he did not refign, though he was of the fame political principles as Mr. Fox and Mr. Buike, he was of the fame opinion with them in regard to the independency of Ameiica, the more equal reprefentation of the people in parliament, and the iegulations neceffary in Ireland· but he did not think the prefent minifter, Lord Shelburne, would act

s   contrary

contrary to thofe principles. As foon as he did, he fhould likewife refign, but not before.

Burke now ftood up and made a moft elegant, though florid fpeech, in praife of the late Marquis of Rockingham As he did not meet with fufficient attention, and heard much talking and many murmurs, he faid, with much vehemence, and a fenfe of injured merit, " *this is not* treatment for fo old a " Member of Parliament as I am, and I will " be heard !"—On which there was immediately a moft profound filence. After he had faid much more in praife of Rockingham, he fubjoined, that with regard to General Conway's remaining in the miniftry, it reminded him of a fable he had heard in his youth, of a wolf, who, on having cloathed himfelf as a fheep, was let into the fold by a lamb, who indeed did fay to him, where did you get thofe long nails, and thofe fharp teeth, mamma? But neverthelefs let him in, the confequence of which was, he murdered the whole flock. Now with refpect to General Conway, it appeared to him, juft as though the lamb certainly did perceive the nails and teeth of the wolf, but notwithftanding, was

fo

fo good-tempeied to believe that the wolf
would change his nature, and become a lamb.
By this, he did not mean at all to reflect on
Lord Shelburn, only of this he was certain,
that the prefent adminiftration was a thoufand
times worfe, than that under Lord North,
(who was prefent)

When I heard Mr. Pitt fpeak, foi the firft
time, I was aftonifhed, that a man of fo
youthful an appearance fhould ftand up at all:
but I was ftill moie aftonifhed to fee how,
while he fpoke, he engaged univerfal attention. He feems to me not to be more than
one and twenty. This fame Pitt is now
minifter, and even Chancellor of the Ex-
chequer.

It is fhocking to a Foreigner, to fee what
violent fatiies on men, rather than on things,
daily appear in the newfpapers, of which
they tell me there are at leaft a dozen, if not
more, publifhed every day. Some of them
fide with the miniftry, and ftill moie I think
with the oppofition. A paper that fhould be
quite impartial, if that were poffible, I appre-
hend, would be deemed fo infipid as to find
no readers. No longer ago than yefteiday, it
wis mentioned in one of thefe newfpapers,

that

that when Fox who is fallen, saw so young a man as Pitt made the minister, he exclaimed with Satan, who, in *Paradise Lost*, on perceiving the man approved by God, called out, " O hateful sight !"

On Thursday the King went with the usual solemnity to prologue the parliament for a stated time. But, I pass this over as a matter that has already been so often described.

I have also, during this period, become acquainted with Baron Grothaus, the famous walker, to whom I had also a letter of recommendation from Baron Groote of Hambro'. He lives in Chesterfield-house, not far from General Paoli, to whom he has promised to introduce me, if I have time to call on him again.

I have suffered much this week from the violent cough I brought with me from the hole in Derbyshire, so that I could not for some days stir. during which time Messrs. Schonborn and Leonhardi have visited me very attentively, and contributed much to my amendment.

I have been obliged to relate as much about my journey out of London, here, as I probably shall in Germany, of all England in general.

general.—To moft people to whom I give an
account of my journey, what I have feen is
quite new. I muft, however, here infert a
few remarks on the elocution, or manner of
fpeaking of this country, which I had forgot
before to write to you.

English eloquence appears to me not to be
nearly fo capable of fo much variety and diffu-
fion as ours is.—Add to this, in their parliamentary fpeeches; in fermons, in the pulpit;
in the dialogues on the ftage; nay, even in
common converfation, their periods at the
end of a fentence are always accompanied, by
a certain fingular uniform fall of the voice;
which, notwithftanding its monotony, has in
it fomething fo peculiar, and fo difficult, that
I defy any foreigner ever completely to
acquire it. Mr. Leonhardi, in particular,
feemed to me in fome paffages, which he repeated out of Hamlet, to have learnt to fink
his voice, in the true English manner, yet
any one might know, from his fpeaking, that
he is not an Englishman. The English place
the accent oftener on the adjectives, than they
do on the fubftantive, which, though undoubtedly the moft fignificant word in any
fentence, has frequently lefs ftrefs laid on it,

than

than you hear'laid on mere epithets.   On the ſtage they pronounce the ſyllables and words extremely diſtinct, ſo that at the Theatres you may always gain moſt inſtruction, in Engliſh elocution and pronunciation.

This kingdom is remarkable for running into dialect; even in London they are ſaid to have one.   They ſay for example, *it a'nt* inſtead of, *it is not*; *I don't know*, for *I do not know*, *I don't know him*, for *I do not know him*; the latter of which phraſes has often deceived me, as I miſtook a negative for an affirmative.

The word *Sir!* in Engliſh has a great va-riety of ſignifications.   With the appellation of *Sir*, an Engliſhman addreſſes his *King*, his *friend*, his *foe*, his *ſervant*, and his dog, he makes uſe of it when aſking a queſtion po-litely; and a Member of Parliament, merely to fill up a vacancy, when he happens to be at a loſs.   *Sir?* In an inquiring tone of voice, ſignifies, what is your deſire?—*Sir!* in an humble tone—gracious ſovereign!—*Sir!* in a ſurly tone, a box on the ear at your ſervice! to a dog it means a good beating.—And in a ſpeech in Parliament, accompanied by a pauſe, it ſignifies I cannot now recollect what it is I wiſh to ſay farther.

I do

I do not recollect to have heard any expreſſion repeated oftener than this *never mind
it!* A porter, one day, fell down, and cut his
head on the pavement : " O, never mind it !"
ſaid an Engliſhman who happened to be paſſing by.   When I had my trunk fetched from
the ſhip, in a boat, the waterman rowed
among the boats, and his boy who ſtood at
the head of his boat, got a ſound drubbing,
becauſe the others would not let him paſs :
" O never mind it !" ſaid the old one, and
kept rowing on.

The Germans who have been here any time,
almoſt conſtantly make uſe of angliciſms,
ſuch as " es will nicht thun," it will not do,
for inſtead of " es iſt nicht hinlanglich," it is
not ſufficient, and many ſuch.   Nay ſome
even ſay, " Ich habe es nicht geminded,"
I did not mind it, inſtead of " ich habe mich
nicht daran erinneſt" " oder daran gedacht,"
I did not recollect it, or I did not think
of it.

You can immediately diſtinguiſh Engliſhmen, when they ſpeak German, by their pronunciation according to the Engliſh manner;
inſtead of " Ich befinde mich wohl," they
ſay

fay " Ich befirmich u'ohl," I am very well, the *W* being as little noticed as *u* quickly founded.

I have often heard, when directing any one in the ftreet, the phrafe: " go down the " ftreet, as far as ever you can go, and afk " any body." Juft as we fay, " every child " can direct you."

I have already noticed in England they learn to write a much finer hand than with us. This probably arifes from their making ufe of only one kind of writing, in which the letters are all fo exact, that you would take it for print.

In general, in fpeaking, reading, in their expreffions, and in writing, they feem, in England to have more decided rules than we have. The loweft man expreffes himfelf in proper phrafes, and he who publifhes a book, at leaft, writes correctly, though the matter be ever fo ordinary. In point of ftile, when they write, they feem to be all of the fame county, profeffion, rank, and ftation.

The printed Englifh fermons are, beyond all queftion, the beft in the world, yet I have fometimes heard fad miferable ftuff from their pulpits.

pulpits.   I have been in some churches where the sermons seemed to have been transcribed or compiled from essays and pamphlets, and the motley composition, after all, very badly put together.   It is said that there are a few in London, by whom some of the English clergy are supposed to get their sermons made for money.

LONDON, 18TH, JULY.

I write to you now for the laft time from London, and, what is ftill more, from St. Catherine's, one of the moft execrable holes in all this great city, where I am obliged to ftay, becaufe the great fhips arrive in the Thames here, and go from hence, and we fhall fail as foon as the wind changes: this it has juft now done; yet ftill, it feems we fhall not fail till to-morrow. To day therefore I can ftill relate to you, all the little that I have farther noticed.

On Monday morning I moved from the Freemafon's Tavern to a Publick-houfe here, of which the mafter, is a German; and where all the Hambro' Captains lodge. At the Freemafon's Tavern, the bill for eight days lodging, breakfaft and dinner, came to one guinea and nine fhillings, and nine pence. Breakfaft, dinner, and coffee, were always with diftinction, reckoned a fhilling each. For my lodging I paid only twelve fhillings a week, which was certainly cheap enough.

At the German's houfe here in St. Catherine's, on the contrary, every thing is more

rea-

reafonable, and you here eat, drink, and lodge, for half-a-guinea a week. Notwith-ftanding, however, I would not advife any body, who wifhes to fee London, to lodge here long, for St. Catherine's is one of the moft out of the way, and inconvenient places in the whole town.

He who lands here, firft fees this miferable narrow dirty ftreet, and this mafs of ill built, old, ruinous houfes; and of courfe forms, at firft fight, no very favourable idea of this beautiful and renowned city.

From Bullftrode ftreet, or Cavendifh-fquare, to St. Catherine's, is little lefs than half a days journey. Neverthelefs Mr Schonborn has daily vifited me fince I have lived here, and I have always walked back half way with him. This evening we took leave of each other, near St. Paul's, and this feparation coft me not a few tears.

I have had a very agreeable vifit this afternoon from Mr. Hanfen, one of the Affiftants to the *Zollner book for all ranks of men*, who brought me a letter from the Rev. Mr. Zoll-ner at Berlin, and juft arrived at London, when I was going away   He is going on bufinefs to Liverpool.   I have, thefe few days

N   paft,

paft, for want of better employment walked
through feveral parts of London that I had not
before feen.   Yefterday I endeavoured to
reach the weft end of the town, and I walked
feveral miles, when finding it was grown quite
dark, I turned back quite tired, without having accomplifhed my end.

Nothing in London makes fo difgufting an
appearance to a Foreigner, as the butchers'
fhops; efpecially in the environs of the Tower.
Guts and all the naftinefs are thrown into the
middle of the ftreet, and caufe an infupporta-
ble ftench.

I have forgot to defcribe the 'Change to you:
this beautiful building is a long fquare, in the
centre of which is an open area where the
merchants affemble.   All round, there are
covered walks fupported by pillars, on which
the name of the different commercial Nations
you may wifh to find are written up, that
among the crowd of people you may be able
to find each other.   There are alfo ftone benches made under the covered walks, which
after a ramble from St. Catherine's, for example, hither, are very convenient to reft yourfelf.

On the walls all kind of hand-bills are ftuck

5   up,

up, among others I read one of fingular contents.   A clergyman exhorted the people
not to affent to the fhameful Act of Parliament for the toleration of Catholics, by fuf-
fering their children, to their eternal ruin, to
be inftructed and educated by them, but rather to give him, an orthodox clergyman, of
the Church of England, this employ, and this
emolument.

In the middle of the area is a ftone ftatue of
Charles the Second.   As I fat here on a bench
and gaz'd on the immenfe crowds that people
London, I thought, that as to mere drefs and
outward appearance thefe here did not feem
to be materially different from our people at
Berlin.

Near the 'Change is a fhop, where, for a
penny or even an halfpenny only, you may
read as many newfpapers as you will.   There
are always a number of people about thefe
fhops, who run over the paper as they ftand,
pay their halfpenny and then go on.

Near the 'Change there is a little fteeple
with a fet of bells, which have a charming tone, but they only chime one or two
lively tunes, though, in this part of the city,

you

you conftantly hear bells ringing in your ears.

It has ftruck me that in London there is no occafion for any elementary works, or prints, for the inftruction of children. One need only lead them into the city and fhew them the things themfelves as they really are. For here it is contrived as much as poffible, to place in view for the public infpection, every production of art, and every effort of induftry. Paintings, mechanifms, curiofities of all kinds, are here exhibited in the large and light fhop windows, in the moft advantageous manner, nor are fpectators wanting, who here and there, in the middle of the ftreet, ftand ftill to obferve any curious performance. Such a ftreet feemed to me to refemble a well regulated cabinet of curiofities.

But the fquares, where the fineft houfes are, diftain and reject all fuch fhews and ornaments, which are adapted only to fhop-keepers' houfes. The fquares, moreover, are not nearly fo crowded, or fo populous, as the ftreets and the other parts of the city. There is nearly as much difference between thefe fquares and the Strand in London, in point of po-

population and buftle, as there is between Mill-bank, and Frederick's-ftadt in Berlin.

I do not at prefent recollect any thing further, my dear friend, worth' your attention, which I can now write to you, except that every thing is ready for our departure to-morrow. I paid Captain Hilkes, with whom I came over from Hambro, four guineas for my paffage and my board in the Cabin. But Captain Braunfchweig, with whom I am to return, charges me five guineas; becaufe provifions, he fays, are dearer in London, than at Hambro. I now have related to you all my adventures and all my hiftory from the time that I took leave of you in the ftreet; my voyage hither with Captain Hilkes excepted. Of this all that I think it neceffary to mention is, that, to my great diffatisfaction it lafted a fortnight, and three days I was fea-fick. Of my voyage back I will give you a perfonal account. And now remember me to Biefter, and farewell till I fee you again.

FINIS.

CPSIA information can be obtained at www.ICGtesting.com
Printed in the USA
BVOW06s1004250315

393296BV00012B/149/P